# HICKORY HILL

## McLean, Virginia

A
**BIOGRAPHY OF A HOUSE
AND THOSE WHO LIVED THERE**

By
Carole L. Herrick

Printed in the United States of America


Published by Higher Education Publications, Inc.
1801 Robert Fulton Drive
Suite 350
Reston, VA 20191-5495


Library of Congress Control Number: 2016937671
Cataloging-in-Publication-Data available from the Library of Congress
Library of Congress CIP data applied for:


ISBN 978-0-914927-76-1

This book is dedicated to the memories of
the families that resided at Hickory Hill

"… houses live their own lives along a time-stream
that's different from the ones upon which their owners
float, one that's slower. In a house, especially an old
one, the past is closer." (Stephen King)

# ACKNOWLEDGEMENTS

Books are not written by the author alone. The ideas and efforts of many others are included, even though they are not seen on the surface. When it comes to books relating to history, research needs to be done. This requires the assistance of librarians, archivists and getting acquainted with others who know the topic. In the course of writing this book I have benefited from the wisdom of many of those individuals. They helped me locate pertinent data and opened doors that led to eliminating legends and producing a book based on facts. Attempting to acknowledge all of those wonderful persons is an impossible task. However, I am especially indebted to Mary Anne Hampton, Steve McAfee and Page Shelp for their wise suggestions and provocative insights, which improved the book in more ways than I can count.

Others who gave generously of their time, for which I am especially grateful, include: Lindsay Aquino, John Q. Barrett, Ron Baumgarten, Heather Bollinger, Linda Blank, Clara Doyle, Alan Dabbiere, Ashley Dabbiere, Laura Faulring, Sharon Glickman, Susan Hellman, Charles Herrick, Martha High, Julie Merrell Harris, Christopher Kennedy, Susan Koehler, Paul Kohlenberger, Katrina Krempasky, Suzanne Levy, Teresa Lindsay, Gina Lofaro, Thomas Loftus III, Pam Lucey, Douglass Sorrell Mackall III, Elaine McHale, Carolyn Cornwell Miller, Congressman James Moran, Melanie Richardson, Virginia Rita, Leo Rocca, Jr., Nancy Smith, Laura Wickstead, and Helen Wirka.

# TABLE OF CONTENTS

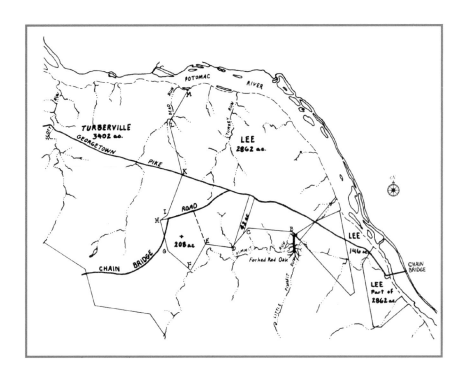

The above map, drawn by Beth Mitchell, shows Thomas Lee's 1719 grant, Chain Bridge and roads with modern names. Langley Fork is where Chain Bridge Road and Georgetown Pike come together. The lower map is the Langley portion of Joseph Berry's 1814 map of McLean.

(Top: Salon*a*) (Lower: Douglass Sorrell Mackall III)

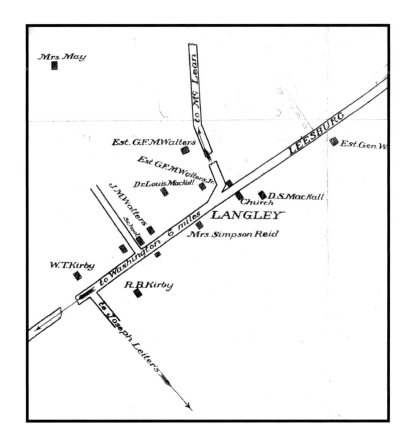

# INTRODUCTION

Several properties in Virginia have been given the name Hickory Hill. Two are particularly significant to the commonwealth due to the families that occupied them and events that occurred there. Both have been placed on the Virginia Register of Historic Places. Each house has its own separate story. This book focuses on the historic home located on Chain Bridge Road in McLean, Fairfax County, and should not be confused with the much older Hickory Hill in Hanover County. Telling a factual story of those who lived in McLean's historic house and grappled with the problems of their day is the intent of this book.

McLean's Hickory Hill was built upon land that was part of a land grant of 2862 acres taken out by Thomas Lee in 1719 from the Northern Neck Proprietary. But it wasn't until ca.1870 that George Franklin Means Walters, the owner of 88 acres of the former grant, built the house near Langley Fork facing Chain Bridge Road. No streak of Puritan modesty restrained him from building the grandest house in the area. He was a master carpenter and his workmanship was not slipshod. The finished product was comfortable and welcoming. It was he who named the house Hickory Hill after the stately old hickory trees that once lined his semicircular driveway. Only a portion of the original 88 acres remain with the house today.

Over the succeeding decades, nine different families have resided at Hickory Hill: Walters, Speer, Fitch, Lyon, Rocca, Jackson, Kennedy (JFK), Kennedy (RFK) and Dabbiere. Each family has made its stamp of change or "improvements" to the property. The original house was a magnificent red brick three story structure built atop a knoll on the site of a former farmhouse. It is thought that the bricks were made using red clay from the back of the property. Brick houses were uncommon in this section of Northern Virginia at that time. The only other brick house in the immediate area was the nearby Federal style Salona, built ca.1800. Walters Hickory Hill was built with a mansard style roof with dormer windows, a roofing style popular in Europe that was gaining acceptance in the United States. It even included a catwalk on top from which a person could see Georgetown, Washington City and the U.S. Capitol building.

The Speer family added the surrounding porch and built the stone wall in front of the house along Chain Bridge Road. Arlington developer Frank Lyon removed the mansard roof, gutted the house, and turned it into a two and half story white brick colonial style residence. The Robert Jacksons enlarged the living room by making one room out of two, included a fireplace in the dining room, installed a recreation room, added more bedrooms, modernized the kitchen, and built a stable to accommodate at least three horses. The Robert Kennedys enlarged the northern wing in 1963 to include a formal dining room, new living room, second floor master bedroom suite, and additional bedrooms for the children. Added to the grounds in back of the house was a tennis court, an Olympic sized swimming pool, a children's pool, and a pool house with changing rooms and a kitchen.

Hickory Hill remained in the hands of the Kennedy family for nearly 50 years. By the time Ethel Kennedy placed the estate for sale in 2003, the house and grounds had fallen into significant disrepair. The listing price at that time was $25,000,000. It's not surprising that the property remained on the market for over six years and had several price reductions. There were multiple issues. Hickory Hill represented a significant piece of Virginia's history and any new construction had to be balanced with the land's storied past. Given the circumstances, restoring the house, grounds and setting to their former grandeur would be a challenging balancing act of blending the old with the new.

Alan and Ashely Dabbiere purchased Hickory Hill through the Hickory Hill Trust in December of 2009. They understood the difficulties they faced and spent a challenging three years in bringing the house back to the quality level it deserved. The inside of the house was gutted and remodeled to accommodate the modernization required to fit today's lifestyle. When finished, the outside facade remained basically the same, although the south wing was enlarged and another section was added to it. The semi-circular driveway is now brick with a vehicular circle in the middle.

The bottom line is that each succeeding family altered Hickory Hill to suit their taste, and today's house bears little resemblance to the residence that Walters built after the Civil War. In any case, the original house may no longer be recognizable, but Hickory Hill remains historic to McLean and Virginia and because of the quality workmanship the Dabbieres put into it, the house should withstand the continuing tests of time.

# CHAPTER I
## The Early Years and the Lee Family

It is hard to decide where to start when writing about a house, particularly one as significant to an area as Hickory Hill. However, it seems prudent to begin its story with the native Indians who settled or roamed the Potomac corridor near the Little Falls of the Potomac. Of course this included the land where Hickory Hill was built centuries later. In the beginning, these were Algonquian-speaking natives who made permanent agricultural settlements along the river's shore. Those on what became the Virginia side of the river were part of the some-what peaceful Powhatan Confederacy. However, by the time Captain John Smith arrived, many of the tribes that had been part of the Powhatan Confederacy were beginning to shift their allegiance to the more aggressive Iroquois to the north. The Iroquois were nomadic hunters and gatherers who used the Potomac River for food and did not build permanent settlements. Smith, with a crew of 14, sailed and paddled up the Potomac in an open barge during June of 1608 only to be stopped by the river's head of navigation at Little Falls.[1] Some proceeded inland by foot on what became the Maryland side of the river and attached a bronze plaque to a tree documenting their travels. Before beginning their descent, the Englishmen traded with the Susquehannocks (Iroquois) in the area where Pimmit Run empties into the Potomac. After returning to Jamestown, Smith's report included that the Potomac River corridor was good for future settlement. Change was coming to the Potomac region. But it was well over a century before this change would begin in the area around the mouth of the Pimmit and northward along the Virginia palisades.

As other Englishmen arrived, colonists began to expand from Jamestown and establish other settlements along the James and Rappahannock Rivers. These settlements were a part of the Virginia government at Jamestown, which operated under a feudal-type arrangement known as the proprietor system. In 1649, the English Stuart King, Charles II, while in exile in France, awarded seven of his loyal followers an extensive land grant in Virginia, known as the Northern Neck Proprietary.[2] After Charles II returned to the throne in 1660, these noblemen were able to exercise their authority and claim their grant. Under the feudal system, the owners of the patent, known as Lord Proprietors, had all the rights of an English court baron and were able to rule over everything in the colony. The settlers were subjects of the proprietors who ruled with absolute authority, as if they were the king. The proprietors could do such things as pass laws with the assistance of a legislative body, establish towns and ports, tax the colonists, raise armies, declare war, build forts and even divide the territory. The patent granted by Charles II was for perpetuity, but the proprietors had to pay an annual fee of six pounds, thirteen shillings, and four pence that was collected at Jamestown the day of the feast of Saint John the Baptist.[3] The proprietors anticipated enlarging their income by collecting quitrents (a form of real estate tax) and from taxing products, such as tobacco, that were exported to the mother country. Over time the make up of the Virginia Proprietorship changed as the proprietors died or the king dismissed them. Since the proprietary grant by Charles II was perpetual, the heirs of the original Northern Neck patent were able to continue as proprietors.

Catherine Culpeper inherited five-sixths of the Northern Neck Proprietary in 1689 at the death of her father Thomas, Second Lord Culpeper, who had bought out the other proprietors.[4] The following year she married Thomas, Fifth Lord Fairfax, who took over the management of her vast Virginia holdings. The Fifth Lord Fairfax died in January of 1710, leaving his widow to manage her five-sixth portion of the proprietorship.[5] Then, four months later, their 16 year old son, Thomas, Sixth Lord Fairfax, inherited the remaining one-sixth portion at the death of his grandmother, Lady Margaret Culpeper.[6] Thus, Lady Catherine became the head proprietor of the Fairfax property. She dismissed Robert "King" Carter as her resident agent in 1711 and replaced him with Edmund Jennings and Thomas Lee.[7] Because Jennings was in London at the time of the appointment, Lee became the active resident agent in Virginia.

Lee held this position for four years and, during his tenure, he took note of land to later patent for himself. When no longer serving Lady Catherine as resident agent, he began buying up land throughout Northern Virginia. In 1719 he purchased 2862 acres along the Potomac River near the Little Falls and called this property Langley after a family estate in Shropshire County, England. This grant was actually two unconnected sections of 2630 and 232 acres each.[8] It was not until 1729 that he was able to purchase the remaining 146 acres that lay between the two parcels, bringing his total acreage at this location to 3008.[9] Pimmit Run ran through a portion of the property. Lee envisioned capturing Virginia's inland trade by establishing a commercial tobacco center where the Pimmit joined the Potomac River. However, it was not until 1742 that he received a license to operate a tobacco inspection station at this location.[10] Lee did not live on the Langley property. Along with his wife Hannah Harrison Ludwell, he lived at Stratford Hall, a plantation house in Westmoreland County that he built in the late 1730s along the banks of the Potomac. They raised a family of six sons and two daughters: Philip Ludwell, Thomas Ludwell, Richard Henry, Francis (Frank) Lightfoot, William, Arthur, Alice and Hannah.[11] Both of the Lees died at Stratford Hall: Hannah, January 25, 1749, and Thomas on November 14, 1750.[12] Their eldest son Philip Ludwell Lee, who was living in England at the time of his father's death, inherited the bulk of his father's estate which included Stratford Hall and, among other items, the 3008 acre Langley tract.

Philip Ludwell Lee returned to Virginia to become the master of Stratford Hall. He married Elizabeth Steptoe in 1763. They had three children; Matilda Ludwell (1764), Flora (1771), and Philip (1775) who died in infancy.[13] Philip Ludwell Lee died unexpectedly in 1775 after a brief illness.[14] The ages of his two daughters were eight and four respectively. The eldest daughter, Matilda, inherited Stratford Hall, but the Langley tract descended to both of his daughters.[15] His will provided that the Langley tract be divided between them. Matilda inherited roughly 1600 acres which included the portion that Hickory Hill was later built upon. Each of the girls married a cousin. In the spring of 1782, 18-year-old Matilda wed Henry, "Light Horse Harry," Lee a dashing cavalry hero of the Revolutionary War, and in 1789 Flora married Ludwell Lee of Belmont in Loudoun County. Both women died before they were thirty years old; Matilda at age 26 on August 16, 1790,[16] and Flora at age 24 in 1795. Matilda and "Light Horse Harry" had three children: Philip Ludwell Lee (1784), Lucy Grymes Lee (1786), and Henry Lee IV (May 2, 1787).

Unfortunately, "Light Horse Harry" had a poor grasp of fiscal realities. He was reckless when it came to matters concerning money and undertook risky investments. This built up staggering financial losses, which quickly began depleting, not only his, but Matilda's vast inheritance. Just before her death, a concerned Matilda protected the inheritance of her three children by having her husband sign a document, dated August 10, 1790, that prevented him from squandering her estate by keeping the remaining properties in trust until her sons were of age.[17] Richard Bland Lee, a younger brother of "Light Horse Harry" and Northern Virginia's first representative to Congress, and Flora's husband Ludwell Lee became the legal representatives of Matilda's estate.[18] Four years after Matilda's death, her eldest son, Philip, died in 1794 at age ten. Her remaining son, Henry Lee, IV ("Black Horse Harry") was now the inheritor of Stratford Hall and, among other items, his mother's 1600 acre portion of the Langley estate.

One of the requirements to receive a patent required that someone live on the property and work the land. From the beginning, the Langley Farm tract was absentee ownership operated by tenant farmers. In 1806, as trustee for Matilda, Richard Bland Lee placed advertisements in newspapers within the District of Columbia seeking someone to rent and operate the Langley Farm. The following item appeared in the *Washington Federalist* on March 15, 1806:

"For the term of Five Years.
To RENT and immedi
ate possession given,

## 1600 Acres of Land,

About 3 miles from Fendall's Mill, near the Little Falls of Potomack. This land is of good quality, and well adapted to wheat and grass, under good inclosures, and having a tolerable dwelling house and other necessary buildings. It is suitable of being divided into several tenements, so as to suit applicants. On the premises is a good blacksmiths shop and tools, and an excellent stand for business.

Tenants may be supplied at a fair price with corn, hay and fodder, carts, wagons and plantation utensils. Also with sundry work horses, mules and oxen. More than 200 bushels of wheat are sown on the premises – which looks well. Mr. George Simpson living on the premises will show the land and other property to applicants.

RICHARD BLAND LEE.

Virginia, Feb. 18, 1806

The above mentioned land is about eight miles from Georgetown by Mason's ferry, and six by the old bridge."[19]

Financial troubles were continual for "Light Horse Harry." Matilda's attempt to keep the Langley Farm out of the hands of her husband and into those of her son failed. Henry Lee IV reached age 21 on May 2, 1808. A little over one month later, on June 7, 1808, "Light Horse Harry" and his son Henry sold the 1600 acre Langley Farm to Richard Bland Lee for $25,000.[20] It does not appear that Matilda's son, Henry, received much, if anything, of his inheritance in this transaction. The purpose of the sale was to aid "Light Horse Harry" in eliminating his debts. At the time of his purchase, Richard

Bland Lee, and his wife Elizabeth Collins, lived at Sully Plantation, an estate of over 1000 acres situated in Western Fairfax County.

Elizabeth Collins Lee inherited a house and lot in Philadelphia upon the death of her father, Stephen Collins, a Quaker merchant. Along with her husband, she sold the house and lot to her brother, Zaccheus Collins, on July 18, 1808. Richard Bland Lee, who was beginning to encounter financial pressures from assisting his older brother, wanted his wife to have something of her own in lieu of the Philadelphia property. Thus, also on July 18, Richard Bland Lee, and his wife Elizabeth, sold 300 of the 1600 Langley Farm acres that lay on the south side of the Falls Bridge Road at a price of $3000 to the Reverend William Maffitt, whose role was to reconvey the land back solely to Elizabeth Lee. The following day, July 19, 1808, Maffitt transferred the 300 acres back to Elizabeth Lee; this deed did not include her husband.[21]

Even though Richard Bland Lee assisted his older brother by coming to his financial rescue and purchasing the Langley Farm, it was not enough. "Light Horse Harry" Lee's irresponsibility in monetary matters continued. About six months after acquiring the Langley tract, Elizabeth and Richard Bland Lee came to "Light Horse Harry's" rescue once again by mortgaging the 1600 acre Langley Farm along with 529 acres of their Sully plantation, where they resided. In this case, "Light Horse Harry" was indebted to Bushrod Washington, a nephew of George Washington, for the sum of $10,034.28. As security to pay off "Light Horse Harry's" debt, the Lees mortgaged the two properties, but were allowed to continue using and managing both of them. The contract was a deed of trust executed on January 9, 1809, and due by March 1, 1814. This allowed a little over five years for the debt to be repaid, which included interest that was to be paid annually. All rents collected from the tenants at Langley Farm were to be turned over to the trustees and used to pay down the $10,034.28 debt. Upon the expiration of the tenants lease at Langley Farm, Richard Bland Lee was at liberty to renew them as long as they did not exceed five years. Henry Smith Turner, of Jefferson County, Thomas Blackburn, of Fairfax County, and Bushrod Washington, Jr., of Westmoreland County, were named as the trustees of the mortgage.[22]

Richard Bland Lee acquired financial troubles of his own and was struggling to work them out, but the added debt burden incurred for assisting his brother proved too much. Not only was he threatened with the mortgage foreclosure of Langley and Sully, but William Herbert, a banker and former mayor of Alexandria, had three judgments against him. To raise the necessary funds to satisfy these judgments, interest, and costs, the Lees found it necessary to sell their Sully plantation and a portion of the Langley Farm. The Sully Plantation was sold to Francis Lightfoot Lee II, a son of Richard Henry Lee, on February 1, 1811, for $18,000.[23] The purchase agreement for Sully stipulated that the buyer (Francis Lightfoot Lee II) would pay Bushrod Washington $7450 from the sale in order to clear the debt Elizabeth and Richard Bland Lee still owed him.[24] The Lees then sold 466 acres of the Langley tract that lay on the south side of the Little Falls Road to Herbert for $6187.85 on May 10, 1811.[25] Often it was difficult for the wife to travel to the county courthouse to be present at the conveyance of the deed and, so, justices of the county, where the transaction took place, were appointed to go to the wife and obtain her signature. They would meet with the wife apart from her husband so that it was clear that he was not pressing her to sign something against her will and, when satisfied she was signing of her own free will, they would obtain her signature. This was the case with Elizabeth Lee. Three justices in Fairfax County, John Ricketts, George Summers and Richard Scott traveled and met privately with her before she put her signature on the deed.[25] This suggests that the Lees had taken care of the loan to Herbert prior to the sale, and both Bushrod Washington and Bushrod Washington, Jr., a trustee of the mortgage, granted release of the acreage.

Richard Bland Lee was now free from debt, but at a huge cost; he would never live the life-style that he formally enjoyed. Why the Lees gave up Sully and held onto the remaining forested land that comprised the Langley tract is unclear. Sully was a functioning plantation with a fine house in which they lived, but it was in the midst of wilderness and at least a day's carriage ride into Georgetown, Washington City or Alexandria. They were basically isolated from the "theater of action." Perhaps they intended to relocate sometime in the future and build on the Langley land. Whatever the case, the Lees moved to Alexandria and lived there briefly, before purchasing Strawberry Vale on January 15, 1812, from Theodoric Lee for $19,000.[26] Strawberry Vale was a 687 acre tract located on the Falls Bridge Road, not too far from the road that led from Alexandria to Leesburg (today's Route 7), and it included an existing farmhouse. Apparently Herbert had no interest in living at the Langley Farm, renting it out or to provide himself with another source of income. It appears that he simply wanted to collect what was due him regarding the three judgments he had against the Lees. He held the property for over a year before placing an advertisement in the *Alexandria Gazette* that the 466 acre Langley Farm was for sale. The announcement was dated November 15, 1811:

"FOR SALE.
A valuable Tract of Land in Fairfax County.

Containing, four hundred and sixty six acres, and situated on the road leading from the Bridge over the river Potomac, at the Little Falls, to the upper country, distant from George Town and the City of Washington four miles, and from Alexandria ten miles.

On this tract is a comfortable dwelling house, and out houses, a young thriving orchard of the choicest fruits, a good garden paled in, and a spring of fine water, that has never been known to fail in the driest season, near the house --- there is a good proportion of it in wood, and a good meadow may be made at a little expense --- the soil is well adapted to Plaister, which can be bro.' by water to the landing at the Little Falls, where there is an extensive merchant mill to grind it, and will leave but about two miles of land carriage. One third of the purchase money must be paid in hand, the other two thirds in two annual payments, to carry interest from the date if not punctually paid.

For further terms apply to the subscriber in Alexandria.
Possession will be given at Christmas.

William Herbert.

November 11."[27]

5

On March 10, 1812, the Reverend William Maffitt purchased 466 acres of Thomas Lee's original Langley patent from William and Sarah Herbert at a price of $6058.[28] This property lay on the south side of the Falls Bridge Road: it was a portion of this acquisition upon which Hickory Hill was later built. On that same day, he also acquired 42 additional acres of land held by Elizabeth and Richard Bland Lee for $420.[29] The smaller parcel was adjacent to the land Maffitt purchased earlier that day from the Herberts. Maffitt was now the landlord of 508 acres on the Falls Bridge Road. This left the Lees with roughly 1100 undeveloped Langley Farm acres.

On June 2, 1608, Captain John Smith and a small crew left Jamestown on the first of two voyages to explore the Chesapeake Bay. Their barge entered the Potomac River on June 16 and stopped at several Indian villages, both hostile and friendly, before reaching the head of navigation at Little Falls on June 24. They were the first group of Englishmen to view the Northern Virginia area.      (Virginia State Library)

In 1609 Catherine Culpeper received title to a five-sixth portion of the Northern Neck Proprietary upon the death of her father, Thomas, Second Lord Culpeper; her mother, Margaret Lady Culpeper, held the remaining one-sixth portion. The following year Catherine married Thomas, Fifth Lord Fairfax of Cameron, who managed her interest in the proprietary. By this marriage the Fairfax family acquired the Northern Neck Proprietary.
(Fairfax County Public Library Archival Division)

After serving as resident agent for Lady Catherine Fairfax, Thomas Lee was able to make use of his knowledge and acquired a great deal of land in Virginia. Among his holdings was a 1719 grant of 2862 acres near the Little Falls of the Potomac. He added 146 acres to this piece in 1729, bringing his total acreage at the falls to 3008. He named this property Langley after an ancestral estate in England. Lee never lived on the Langley land, but resided at Stratford Hall in Westmoreland County.          (Stratford Hall)

Henry "Light Horse Harry" Lee (right) was a grandson of Henry Lee, a brother of Thomas Lee. He achieved fame as a gallant cavalry officer at the Battle of Paulus Hook during the American Revolution. Lee married his cousin Matilda, the daughter of Philip Ludwell Lee. "Light Horse Harry" speculated in land and was constantly facing financial woes. Matilda died at a young age, leaving the Langley Farm to their son Henry Lee IV. "Light Horse Harry" later married Anne Hill Carter. Their fifth child gained fame as the Confederate General, Robert E. Lee.
(Library of Congress)

The owners of the Sully Plantation, Richard Bland Lee (above), and his wife Elizabeth Collins (below) purchased the Langley Farm in 1808. Lee was driven into severe debt trying to assist his older brothers, Henry "Light Horse Harry" and Charles, with their financial difficulties.                    (Virginia State Library)

SKETCH BY MARIANO ECKERT

The above sketch by Margaret Eckert depicts Sully as it may have appeared after its completion in 1795. Elizabeth and Richard Bland Lee were forced to sell the plantation in 1811 to alleviate financial troubles they incurred when assisting "Light Horse Harry" Lee with his debts.     (*Sully*)

This is a photo of a declining Strawberry Vale ca.1782 taken by J. Harry Shannon in 1916. Strawberry Vale, located on the Falls Bridge Road, consisted of 687 acres when the Lees purchased it from Theodoric Lee in 1812. The house was torn down in 1958 for the development of Westpark Industrial Park and the construction of Interstate 495.

(Fairfax County Public Library Archival Division)

# CHAPTER 2
## Maffitt and Salona

Unlike the Lees and the Turbervilles, Maffitt did not come from Virginia's aristocracy. He hailed from gentry in Cecil County, Maryland, where his father was a justice of the peace, elder in the Presbyterian Church, owner of a flourishing farm, mill operator, and a major under George Washington during the American Revolution.[1] It is thought that Maffitt studied theology, but records cannot be found to indicate if, or where, he attended school. On October 9, 1794, he was licensed by the New Castle Presbytery: at that time, it appears that he was a teacher at the Wilmington Academy. On April 7, 1795, Maffitt was sent to the Baltimore Presbytery, with residency in Alexandria.[2] In 1798 he was transferred to a Presbyterian missionary in Alexandria, where he was a schoolmaster at the Alexandria Academy, an affluent school for boys that taught many things such as history, the classics and English grammar. Maffitt joined the Masons in 1799, becoming a member of Masonic Lodge No 22. On December 13 of that same year, George Washington, also a member of Lodge No 22, died at his home Mount Vernon. Memorial services were held throughout America. Four memorial services took place at the Presbyterian Meeting House in Alexandria, prior to Washington's official funeral and internment at Mount Vernon. At the Presbyterian Meeting House the Reverend James Muir delivered one of the memorial sermons: the other three speeches were offered by Revered Thomas Davis, an Episcopalian; Reverend James Tolleson, a Methodist; and Reverend Maffitt, a Presbyterian. A multitude of citizens, that included Maffitt, then proceeded to Mount Vernon and gathered around Washington's grave site. The actual funeral service was performed by the Reverend Davis, Rector of Alexandria's Christ Church, and the ceremonies of the Masonic fraternity were conducted by Reverend Muir, Chaplain of Alexandria's Lodge No 22, and by physician Elisha Dick, Worshipful Master of the Lodge.[3]

Maffitt married Henrietta (Harriotte) Lee Turberville, the widow of George Richard Lee Turberville on May 5, 1803, in the City of Alexandria.[4] Henrietta was the daughter of Richard Henry Lee, one of two sons of Thomas and Hanna Lee, who signed the Declaration of Independence. After her husband's death in 1802, Henrietta had remained at her residence, Leeton, a Turberville plantation located in western Fairfax County. Maffitt moved into Leeton where he lived with his wife, and her three Turberville children: Cornelia, Richard and George Richard Lee Turberville II. The Maffitt's first daughter Ann Lee was born on March 23, 1804. Shortly thereafter, Maffitt resigned from the Alexandria Academy where he had been the principal. Henrietta's older brother Thomas Lee had been the legal guardian[5] of her three children until his death in 1802.[6] Maffitt was then appointed the legal guardian of the three Turberville children and was required to keep a detailed report of all expenditures.[7] Sadly, Henrietta died on March 16, 1805, shortly after the birth of their second child, Harriotte. This was less than two years after her second marriage: Maffitt was left a widower with the demanding task of raising five young children.

Maffitt continued to reside at Leeton. It was not his property, but that of his three stepchildren and, so, he must have found it awkward remaining there. Included in the

Turberville expenditure accounts is a line item showing that Maffitt began to pay an annual rent on April 12, 1805, to the Turberville heirs for continuing to live at Leeton.[8] Maffitt remarried. This time he wed Ann Beale Carter Carter, the widow of Charles B. Carter, who died in 1807 at his estate Mount Atlas in Prince William County.[9] Charles was the son of Charles Carter of Shirley Plantation: Ann was the daughter of Winifred Beale and Robert Wormeley Carter of Sabine Hall near Richmond. Ann had seven children, and they came with her when she entered the household of Maffitt, which already had five children. According to the 1810 Census, the couple was living in Fairfax County: this would be at Leeton. Listed were 12 children under 16 years of age: they would be the three stepchildren from Henrietta's Turberville marriage, two children from Maffitt's marriage to Henrietta, and seven stepchildren that came with Ann Carter. Maffitt is also shown as having 53 slaves. A son William Maffitt II, was born to the couple in 1811.

Soon after purchasing the Langley property, Maffitt, along with his large family, moved into the stately brick mansion located on the 466 acre section. Whether the house was called Salona at this time is unclear, but after the Maffitts moved in, the estate was always known as Salona. At that time the surrounding area was little more than wilderness. What Maffitt bought was a self-sustaining farm that relied upon hired hands and slaves to keep it functioning. Until this time, the brick house was the first dwelling of any significance that a traveler encountered after crossing the Chain Bridge and moving up the Falls Bridge Road into Virginia; Salona was on the south side of the road, about three miles from the bridge. It wasn't until the 1812 marriage of Matilda Lee and Richard Love that another substantial residence was built in the area. This was Rokeby, a farmhouse built on the north side of the Falls Bridge Road, but nearer to the Potomac River. The Rokeby land had remained untouched for generations. It was the divided portion of Thomas Lee's 1719 grant that was inherited by Flora Lee after the death of her father, Philip Ludwell Lee. Flora died at a young age and her daughter, Matilda, who was named after her sister Matilda, inherited the property. The farmhouse was completed in 1813.[10] There were at least two other residential dwellings nearby. One was Benvenue, a stone house ca.1757, that was within sight distance of Salona and faced the Falls Bridge Road and the other was Minor's Hill, a few miles away in the direction of Falls Church. A few other dwellings were scattered about the immediate area that were made of logs or clapboard, but none of the existing homes compared to the stately red brick Salona. It was the "crown jewel" of this particular part of Northern Virginia. In the Court Order Book for Fairfax County Road Orders, Salona was often referred to as the "Red House" suggesting that it may have been constructed during the time of Philip Ludwell Lee's ownership of the 3008 acre tract.[11]

A few months after Maffitt purchased Salona, the United States declared war against Great Britain. Known as the War of 1812, it had little impact on residents of the District of Columbia and the surrounding area until the summer of 1814 when, after raiding towns throughout the Chesapeake Bay, the British advanced towards the nation's capital city. On the afternoon of August 24, 1814, British troops defeated American militia forces at Bladensburg, Maryland, leaving the city vulnerable for the British to enter and destroy. Those who had not already vacated the nation's capital before the

American lines collapsed suddenly found themselves in a desperate situation that required a hasty exit from the city. President James and First Lady Dolley Madison escaped capture by fleeing into the countryside of Virginia. They did not leave the city at the same time, but took separate routes across the Potomac. Dolley bravely remained at the President's House (known today as the White House) listening to the sounds of cannon fire at Bladensburg until she learned that a retreat had been ordered.[12] After seeing to the safety of the full-length portrait of George Washington,[13] she hastened to Bellevue, the Georgetown home of Charles Carroll, where she joined a contingent of people awaiting the arrival of her husband.[14]

President Madison, who had been on the field of battle, returned to the President's House after his wife had departed. He remained for about an hour, while preparations were made for his departure. While waiting, he sent two messages to Bellevue. The first note requested that everyone meet him at Foxall's Foundry and the second simply said to meet him on the other side.[15] After leaving the President's House, Madison took the Georgetown Ferry across the river to Mason's Island and then traveled across the causeway into Virginia.[16] Where he ended up that night is unclear: it is thought that he found refuge with the Maffitts at Salona.[17] After receiving the second note, Dolley, in company with numerous persons, hastened to the Georgetown Ferry, only to learn that the president had already crossed the river. She then proceeded down what today is Canal Road, crossed the Chain Bridge, moved up the very steep Chain Bridge Hill, and stopped at the Love's farmhouse Rokeby, the residence of very good friends.[18] There she spent the night, while the British set fire to public buildings that included the Capitol and, her residence, the President's House.

The following morning, Dolley left Rokeby and stopped at Salona as she was traveling further inland. Ann Maffitt was also an acquaintance of hers. The president returned to Wren's Tavern in Falls Church to get updates about the location of the American forces and the possibility of General William Winder initiating a counterattack. While receiving a guard of two dragoons, Madison told Captain George Graham that he expected to find Dolley at Mr. Maffitts, and, turning his horse, headed in that direction.[19] Whether the Madisons' were together at Salona is unclear. However, Dolley left Salona early in the afternoon and journeyed to Wiley's Tavern, located on the road that led from Alexandria to Leesburg. She reached the tavern around 3:00 p.m., just as a hurricane force thunderstorm arrived.[20] The president left Salona for Wiley's Tavern in mid-afternoon unprepared for the approaching horrific storm, but was able to receive shelter in a home near today's Tysons Corner.[21] After the storm subsided, he continued on to Wiley's, where he joined Dolley.

Madison remained at Wiley's just long enough to have some refreshments and take a much needed rest. He left with several companions about midnight to cross the Potomac using Conn's Ferry in anticipation of joining the American forces at Montgomery Court House.[22] When reaching the ferry site, the ferryman informed everyone that the river was too dangerous to cross due to the earlier horrific storm.[23] Where he slept the second night out of the city is unknown; it is possible that he spent the remainder of the night in the home of the ferryman. The following afternoon, August 26, everyone was ferried across the river and Madison ended the day in Brookville, Maryland, at the home of Caleb and Henrietta Bentley.[24] The president was informed the next day that the British had evacuated the city the evening of August 25 and that it was safe to return. That afternoon, August 27, Madison, in the company of Secretary of State James Monroe and Attorney General Richard Rush, returned to the still smoldering capital.[25] Since his residence was destroyed, he went to the home of Dolley's sister Anna and her husband Richard Cutts.[26] Dolley stayed at the tavern after the president departed. However, rather than proceeding further inland the next day, she headed back towards the city for Minor's Hill in Falls Church.[27] There she spent two nights before returning to Washington City on Sunday, August 28.[28]

For the Langley area, the excitement created by the fleeing president, his wife and other government officials was over once the Madisons returned to the capital city. The humid Potomac summer was drawing to a close and the rigorous chore-filled daily grind activities necessary to maintain a working farm went on as usual. But it was not long before the routine began to change regarding Maffitt's Turberville stepchildren. Tragedy struck in June of 1815 when Richard drowned in the Potomac River during a swimming/bathing party while visiting his aunt, Matilda, at nearby Rokeby.[29] This was followed by his brother, George, acquiring typhoid fever (the date is unknown) and completely loosing his hearing. Since the young man could not hear, his ability to speak was limited; he became a deaf mute. In 1818 George was sent to "The Asylum," in Connecticut for treatment and Maffitt advanced the young man $200 for travel, board and tuition.[30] However, George often returned to Salona for vacations. In February of 1817, Cornelia left the Maffitt household to marry Charles Calvert Stuart in Alexandria.[31] The couple built a house on a portion of the Leeton tract approximately two miles east of Sully in Fairfax County that had been patented by Cornelia's great-grandfather, George Turberville, in 1727. The house was named Chantilly, after the Westmoreland County estate of Cornelia's grandfather Richard Henry Lee.[32]

Unfortunately, Maffitt was not particularly adroit at operating a farm. The scope of maintaining such a large scale operation may have been more than he anticipated. His financial situation began to slowly decline and he eventually found it necessary to borrow money from one of his sisters Margaret Maffitt Whann, who lived in Georgetown. On November 1, 1823, Whann loaned her brother $6000 and, as collateral, Maffitt mortgaged the 466 acre Salona farm to her.[33] The loan, plus interest, was to be repaid by August 10, 1829. But before the entire obligation was returned, Maffitt passed away at Salona on March 2, 1828,[34] leaving an outstanding debt of $3716.54 still due his sister.[35] He left no will and, by this time, had little in the way of personal property.[36] Unfortunately, Virginia did not keep death certificates prior to 1858 and there are no family records to indicate how, or from what, Maffitt died. He was very conscientious about his personal finances and those of his stepchildren. The fact that Maffitt died intestate, leaving Ann with a large financial burden, suggests that his death may have been sudden and unexpected.

Ann continued to reside at Salona, and the house become known as the Dower Mansion.[37] Her life must have been difficult: she had to manage the slaves, maintain the farm operations and see to the welfare of the remaining children. However, the biggest difficulty she faced was the outstanding debt owed her sister-in-law and, no matter how hard she tried, she just could not meet the obligations of the mortgage. The remaining debt was still due on August 10, 1829. Robert C. Jackson took over the task of overseeing the administration of Maffitt's estate and, during 1828, the court appointed four persons to take an inventory and appraise Maffitt's personal property and slaves.[38] Not including slaves, the value of Maffitt's personal estate was assessed at $1588.89.[39] Even though this assessment was conducted in 1828, Maffitt's estate was not filed with the Fairfax County Court until 1832.[40] Relatives tried to help Ann financially by purchasing some of her husband's personal property and slaves at a sale that took place on May 20, 1829. George Turberville, Elizabeth Carter, John Hill Carter, Reverend Thomas Balch, and Thomas ap Catesby Jones were among the purchasers.[41]

The debt owed Whann was reduced with the help of the relatives, but the mortgage was still not completely paid. Whann was also a widow. Her husband Captain David Whann died unexpectedly of sunstroke in 1813 while reviewing troops on the parade ground in the District of Columbia and she was left with two children. She had financial problems of her own and was desirous of seeing that the mortgage be repaid. Even though her husband had been a naval captain, the government would not compensate her for his untimely death.[42] She was not unreasonable in her endeavor for payment of her brother's loan and finally instituted a chancery suit against Maffitt's heirs; on April 1, 1831, the 466 acre Salona property, was offered for sale at public auction under the authority of the Court of Fairfax County. Whann must have thought that the best way to get back her money was to actually own Salona. Her agent was her son-in-law, the Reverend James McVean. He purchased Salona for her at an auction held at the Fairfax Court House on April 18, 1831, by bidding $2650.[43] Whann had additional expenses of $110.90 to cover the fees of the auction and the cost of the suit against the heirs which would be taxed by the clerk of Fairfax County before the property was turned over to her. Thus, the purchase price amounted to $2760.09.[44] The additional expenses were paid and on October 18, 1831, the 466 acre Salona farm was conveyed to Whann.[45]

In spite of all of the turmoil, the widow Maffitt continued living at Salona. The issue of her residency was resolved a few years later when, on July 29, 1835, Ann, along with her husband's three heirs, Ann Lee Maffitt, Harriott Maffitt Post, and William Maffitt, Jr., sold Whann the right of dower in Salona and the smaller 42 acre tract. Whann paid the widow Maffitt $725 "And that in consideration thereof the said Ann shall release her right of Dower as well to the said Tract called 'Salona' as to the said Smaller Tract of Land. And that the said Heirs shall release to the said Margaret all their right title and claim in Law and Equity to the said larger Tract, and Convey to her the smaller tract adjoining it hereto."[46]

---

Elizabeth Carter and John Hill Carter were children of Ann's by her first marriage. Reverend Thomas Balch was the husband of another daughter Susan Carter and Thomas ap Catesby Jones was the husband of her daughter Mary Walker Carter. Jones was a leading naval figure in the 1815 Battle of New Orleans and owned a nearby farm that faced the Georgetown-Leesburg Turnpike named Sharon

Shortly thereafter, the widow Maffitt moved to Fauquier County, Virginia, to live with the family of her daughter Susan Carter and Susan's husband the Reverend Thomas B. Balch.[47] Whann, however, remained in Georgetown and did not relocate across the other side of the Potomac into Virginia. However, she held on to the Salona farm for several years. During this time, the house was occupied by tenants who farmed the land and paid her rent. It wasn't until June 7, 1842, that Whann sold the property. On that date Laura and Chapman Lee, who had recently moved to Alexandria from Connecticut, purchased both the 466 acre Salona farm and the adjoining smaller tract. The price for the combined parcels was $7500.

The Chapman Lees did not keep the Salona tract for long. They began dividing the land and selling off portions starting in 1843 when 100 acres were sold to Henry C. Taylor who had arrived in Virginia from New York state.[48] This was followed in 1845 when a Connecticut resident, Elisha Sherman, purchased 208 acres that included the house Salona for $5421.[49] Shortly thereafter, on November 1, 1845, the Chapman Lees sold 25 acres to William Muse at a price of $500.[50] The Muse purchase lay on the east side of Salona, adjacent to the 208 acre Sherman purchase. On January 1, 1846, George Franklin Means Walters acquired 88.5 acres from the Lees for $1850.50 ($21.00 per acre).[51] It was upon Walter's 88.5 acre acquisition that a house was built along the Falls Bridge Road after the Civil War named Hickory Hill.

During the War of 1812, British regular troops defeated American militia at Bladensburg, Maryland, before entering and setting fire to the capital of the United States. Dolley Madison courageously remained at the President's House until learning that the American lines had fallen. Before escaping into the Virginia countryside she saw to the safety of the full-length portrait of George Washington that remained hanging on the dining room wall. Once Dolley knew the painting would be taken to a place of safety, she left and ended her flight that fiery night at Rokeby, a farm about a mile above the Chain Bridge. She was out of the city four nights. Since the President's House had been destroyed by the British, the Madisons moved into the home of Dolley's sister, Anna, and her husband Richard Cutts, The Madisons remained there until moving into the Octagon House.    (Library of Congress)

James Madison was the fourth President of the United States. On June 18, 1812, he signed a declaration of war against Great Britain. It was an unpopular war. A little over two years later, British forces defeated American militia troops at Bladensburg, Maryland on August 24, 1814.The president and his wife Dolley were forced to separately flee Washington City for the safety of the Virginia countryside. British troops entered the nation's capital city and set fire to its public buildings. It is thought that the president spent that fiery night at Salona, the home of the Reverend William and Ann Carter Carter Maffitt.
(Library of Congress)

The above photograph of the red brick Salona was taken sometime during the late 1970s.
(Fairfax County Public Library Archival Division)

The grave of the Reverend William Maffitt, along with those of members of the Mackall, Jones and Walters families, is located in the cemetery adjacent to the Lewinsville Presbyterian Church in McLean. The tombstone inscription reads: "REV. WILLIAM MAFFITT, DIED AT SALONA, FAIRFAX CO. VA, MAR 2, 1828, AGE 59 YEARS. ERECTED BY HIS AFFECTIONATE WIDOW. (Carole Herrick)

Commodore Thomas ap Catesby Jones was a leading figure in the 1815 Battle of New Orleans. His estate, Sharon, faced the Georgetown-Leesburg Turnpike about two miles west of Langley. Jones married, Mary Walker Carter, a daughter of Ann Maffitt by her first marriage and was one of many who assisted Ann financially through an estate sale in 1829. He is buried in the Lewinsville Cemetery adjacent to the Lewinsville Presbyterian Church. His tombstone is shown below.

(Top: Fairfax County Public Library Archival Division)
(Bottom: Carole Herrick)

19

SALES AT AUCTION.

## Valuable Land for sale.

UNDER the authority of a Decree of the County Court of Fairfax, in the case of Margaret Whann against William Maffitt's heirs, the subscriber will offer for sale, at public auction, *on the third MONDAY in March next* (being Court day) that valuable

*TRACT OF LAND called SALONA* on which the said William Maffit formerly resided, containing

**466 ACRES.**

There are on the premises a large and commodious two story brick

*DWELLING HOUSE,*

With a number of Out-houses, and an ORCHARD of CHOICE FRUIT TREES. The land is in good cultivation, and is situated on the Falls Bridge Turnpike Road, about six miles from Georgetown.

Sale to take place in the front of the Court House of Fairfax County, at ten o'clock P. M  Terms cash.

THOMAS MOSS,
Commissioner.

feb 25—dts

☞ The National Intelligencer will insert the above every other day till sale.

The Salona property was offered for sale at public auction in 1831. Margaret Whann purchased it seeking repayment of a loan given her brother, the Reverend William Maffitt in 1829. The above advertisement appeared in the *Alexandria Gazette* in February of 1831. *(Alexandria Gazette)*

# CHAPTER 3
## Langley's Early Years and the Walters Family

At the time Walters acquired his 88.5 acre property, a community that became known as Langley was beginning to form, developing around the spot where two roads connected to create a "fork in the road." The two roads were the Falls Bridge Road (also called the Court House Road) and the Falls Bridge Turnpike Road. The turnpike road had its start in 1813 when the Falls Bridge Turnpike Company was chartered by Virginia's General Assembly and, by 1827, it had completed a toll road that led from the Chain Bridge to the Alexandria-Leesburg Turnpike at Dranes Tavern.[1] Before the road was finished, the company, in 1820, built a toll house that was located to the east of the intersection and a paid toll keeper to collect revenue for those who passed.[2] This was the first commercial establishment in the Langley area. There was also a weighing station at the fork where farmers were required to weigh their loads before continuing on to the markets in the District of Columbia.[3] The two roads were well used by farmers, drovers, stagecoach drivers and travelers as they proceeded to and from the District of Columbia, but there was little to detain them in the vicinity of the intersection except the requirement to stop and pay the toll.

In 1838, Brooke Mackall, a Georgetown resident, purchased 540 acres of the Langley tract from Elizabeth Lee, and the heirs of her husband, Richard Bland Lee, for $2900.[4] This property roughly began at the fork and ran northwest. Even though Mackall purchased the property, little was done to improve it at that time. He proceeded to enlarge his holding in 1842 by purchasing three separate adjoining tracts of land that totaled 150.5 acres at a price of $600. This was done through a deed of trust for the benefit of his older brother Benjamin F. Mackall and his heirs.[5] At that time Benjamin, a lawyer, who also lived in Georgetown, was the director and former president of the Falls Bridge Turnpike Company.[6] It was several years after the two transactions were completed before Benjamin reconstructed an existing house that stood on the north side of the Falls Bridge Turnpike Road, west of the fork. He named it Langley and eventually relocated to Virginia. The house was rebuilt on a much grander scale than the previous dwelling. It has gone down in area history as the Mansion House of Langley[7] and the place where the two roads joined became known as Langley Fork.

As trade between inland Virginia and the District of Columbia continued to grow, a Loudoun County farmer, named William ("Billy") Means obtained a license on July 18, 1842, to keep a house of private entertainment.[8] Along with his wife Mary, he moved to Langley and opened a tavern on the north side of the turnpike at the fork. The terms tavern, house of private entertainment, inn, ordinary and drover's rest were often used interchangeably. Under Virginia law at that time a license to operate a tavern or house of private entertainment did not permit the licensee to serve alcoholic drinks. The licensee was required to furnish lodging, food and provide the traveler with stableage, pastorage and feed for his horse. Whereas, the requirements to operate an ordinary, or a house of public entertainment, were the same as the tavern, but the licensee could serve spirited beverages if he so desired.[9] The license had to be renewed in the spring of each year and the name for the permit often changed. For instance, Means was issued a license to operate a house of private entertainment from 1842-1847; from 1848-1852 he had a license for an ordinary; from 1853-1856 it was a public entertainment license; and 1857-1860 he once again had a license for a house of private entertainment.[10] Why Means, and his wife Mary, left Loudoun County for Fairfax County to operate a tavern is not known. Prior to relocating in Langley, Means had been a slave-owning farmer.[11] It is interesting to note that Means never did own the property at Langley upon which the tavern operated, but leased it from the Mackall family.[12]

As the Langley community began to grow, a post office was established on October 26, 1846. It operated from inside the tavern, which also included a general store.[13] Means was appointed Langley's first post master, a position he continuously held until 1858. At the time Means received the appointment, one of his sons, Lewis Means, was already operating a post office at Prospect Hill, beginning on November 29, 1844. Prospect Hill was only a few miles further up the Falls Bridge Turnpike Road.[14]

Means was the father-in-law of George F. M. Walters, who married his daughter, Mary Means, in 1845.[15] After purchasing the 88.5 Langley property, George and Mary Walters, were ready to take up residency in Langley and begin a family. Over the years many have participated in events that left a lasting imprint on the area, but it was the families of Walters and Mackall that became the principle "movers and shakers" in Langley.

As one of six children, George Walters grew up in Fairfax County in an area south of the Alexandria-Leesburg Turnpike (Route 7), known today as Wolf Trap Run. His parents James and Sarah Brown Walters were Quakers. They came to the county from Waterford, in Loudoun County, after purchasing the 663 acre tract known as Mount Salus from Stewart Brown in 1811.[16] The Walters family moved into an existing mansion house on the property, renaming it Ivy Hill, and undertook grist milling operations along Wolf Trap Run.[17] The mill was located along the stream in the area of today's Beulah and Brown's Mill Roads and for the next 90 years it was known as Walters' Mill.[18] The remaining land was farmed and even though James Walters was of the Quaker faith, he occasionally owned a few slaves.[19] James Walters died intestate on August 5, 1840, and in September of 1842, appointed commissioners divided his real estate into lots amongst his heirs. His widow, Sarah, received the Dower Lot of 115.5 acres that contained Ivy Hill[20] and each of their children received a one-sixth portion of the remaining Mount Salus tract. In the division, George was awarded Lot 5 consisting of 105 acres and a farmhouse. Lot Number 4, containing 182 acres went to his older brother William.[21] It is assumed that after George wed Mary Means the couple moved into the existing farmhouse on his portion of the division where they lived until relocating to Langley. Walters was a carpenter by trade. After purchasing the Langley property, he built a small frame house on the land facing the Falls Bridge Road and, when finished, the couple moved into it and began raising their family.[22]

Like his father, George Walters was of the Quaker religion and known for using "Thee" and "Thou" when speaking. However, the tiny hamlet of Langley was not a Quaker community: in fact, there were no Quaker meetings in Langley during his entire lifetime. This had also been the situation with his parents. There were no Quaker meetings near their Mount Salus property. The nearest was the Fairfax Monthly Meeting in Waterford and it was nearly a 30 mile journey to attend services there. James Walters continued his membership with the Fairfax Meeting, but joined the local Methodist Society for additional moral and social guidance regarding his family. He was one of the original trustees who organized a nearby Methodist Episcopal Church. Eli and Margaret Offutt in 1836 conveyed two acres of land to seven trustees, one of which was James Walters. The Union Meeting House was already on the property. It was to be repaired and turned into a place of worship for the members of the Methodist Episcopal Church. The new church became known as the Old Union Church.[23] It was located on Towlston Road at the spot where the Bethel Regular Baptist Church stands today.

After moving to Langley, the Walters family began worshiping at Nelson's Chapel, a Methodist congregation that met in a small structure on property owned by William Nelson, the owner of two mills along Pimmit Run.[24] As membership in Nelson's Chapel grew, its congregation split over the issue of slavery. Walters, along with William W. Ball, Richard Hirst, John Gantt and Weathers Smith, was appointed to be a trustee to help organize another place in which to worship, to be known as the Methodist Episcopal Church South.[25] The women connected with the new church held a fair on September 16, 1852, to raise funds for erecting a house of worship. The fair was held in a lightly wooded area that was known as The Grove. This was a portion of Walters' property that lay directly opposite the tavern/post office of Means. The *Alexandria Gazette* printed the following advertisement on September 3, 1852:

"LADIES FAIR. – The Ladies connected with the Methodist E. Church, South, (Fairfax Circuit) will hold a FAIR, on *Thursday, 16th of September*, in the beautiful Grove, belonging to Mr. George F. M. Walters, opposite the Langley Post Office, (Mr. Wm. Mean's Tavern) on the Falls Bridge Turnpike, to aid in the erection of a house of worship; which is now in progress, near Mrs. Young's toll gate. There will be provided a plentiful DINNER and other refreshments usual on such occasions, together with many useful and fancy articles. The citizens of the District, Alexandria, and the County of Fairfax who feel disposed to aid in this laudable effort to extend the cause of the Redeemer, with all those who would like to spend a pleasant day, in this delightful Grove, are cordially invited to attend. Every effort will be made on the part of those connected with the FAIR, to make the day pass pleasantly to all."

A one-half acre piece of land was conveyed by Benjamin Mackall, and his brother Richard, to be used for the "benefit of the Methodist Episcopal Church South as a place of public worship and for holding Sabbath School and Prayer Meetings."[26]The new church was constructed on the north side of the Falls Bridge Turnpike Road, slightly west of the fork and the first service in the new building was held in 1858.[27] Black Methodists in the area worshiped upstairs in the new church.[28] The building, with significant alternations, still stands today, and is occupied by the Country Day School.

The Grove and the tavern became community gathering places for meetings, auctions, and many other activities, that included not only residents of the neighborhood, but citizens throughout Northern Virginia. A public meeting was held at the tavern on the afternoon of October 20, 1852, "for the purpose of taking more effectual action to ensure the reconstruction of a bridge at the Little Falls of the Potomac in lieu of the one carried away by the freshet in April last."[29] This was the fifth bridge that spanned the Potomac River near the Little Falls. It was no longer a chain bridge, but the name Chain Bridge continued. The bridge had been swept away in a violent spring flood on April 20, 1852. Langley residents and inland Virginia farmers were dependent upon the bridge to access Georgetown and the City of Washington and they were fearful that another bridge would not be built at that location. The bridge was replaced, but it was done in stages, and it was not until early 1858 that it was completed in its entirety.[30]

The "Always Ready Club," used Walters' Grove for many of their barbecues. This was an organization that consisted of local citizens who attempted to keep the area informed about local and national issues. The club organized in August of 1848 at Freeland in Nelson's School House[31] (Nelson's Chapel) and held its first barbecue the following month with distinguished speakers and patriotic music at that location. Over 600 people attended.[32] After that, the event was held in Walters' Grove. On October 20, 1852, *The National Intelligencer* printed:

> "FREE BARBEQUE --- There will be a free Barbeque given by the "Always Ready Club,' on Tuesday, the 20th of October instant, in the grove of George F. M. Walters, Esq., at the Liberty and Union Pole, near the tavern of WILLIAM MEANS, at Langley two miles above the Chain Bridge Ferry. Good speakers, and good music will be in attendance, and plenty for all. Come, one and all. Speaking to commence at 10 o'clock A. M."

Interest in religious activities reinforced a growing preoccupation with questions concerning moral issues. The consumption of alcohol was considered to be one of the worst vices. Temperance organizations formed across the nation advocating temperance rather than complete abstinence in the use of intoxicating liquor. Religious organizations tried to educate everyone about the evils of "spirited beverages" and sponsored parades, and held festivals: Walters' Grove was often used for such activities. A festival of the Langley Division Sons of Temperance was held at The Grove on August 7, 1852. Seven to eight hundred people attended the free event, ate food, drank non-spirited beverages and listened to several notable personalities addressing the evils of consuming liquor. The *Alexandria Gazette* described the afternoon:

> "The temperance festival at Langley, in Fairfax county, on Saturday, was a grand affair. There were present not less than seven or eight hundred ladies and gentlemen. A sumptuous dinner was prepared, to which all present were invited free of charge. During the day a number of very interesting addresses were delivered by Rev. Mr. Cox of Georgetown, Mr. Savage, of Washington, and others. The beautiful banner was presented by Mrs. Langdon, on the part of the ladies."[33]

Over time Walters acquired additional property in the Langley area. He began in January of 1853 by purchasing 20 acres from Samuel and Sarah Randall for $500 ($25 per acre) which lay opposite his home on the other side of the Falls Bridge Road.[34] The following year he purchased an additional 40 acres of land for $1600 ($40 per acre) from John and Eliza Younglove.[35] This parcel began at the southeast corner of the Falls Bridge Road and the road that led to Alexandria (today's Potomac School Road). Then on December 15, 1858, he acquired slightly more than four acres from Edmund Wilson for

$150 ($37.50 per acre) that lay on the north side of the Falls Bridge Turnpike Road to the east of the fork.[36] Walters' land holdings at Langley now totaled 152 acres.

Walters completed building a substantial dwelling at the southeast corner of Langley Fork ca.1856; the value of his real estate increased substantially at this time as shown on the 1857 Fairfax County land records.[37] This structure has gone down in Northern Virginia's history as the Langley Ordinary, but Walters' intension was that it serve as a drover's rest. The license Means obtained in 1842 to operate a tavern was for a house of private entertainment; it did not allow him to serve liquor. Unlike a tavern, an ordinary was a place of hospitality that served as a drover's rest and, if licensed, could offer food, drink and spirited beverages. Because of Walters' temperance background, it seems unlikely that his ordinary offered alcoholic beverages. It is probable that in the beginning Means operated both the tavern and the ordinary. However, before the outbreak of the American Civil War, Means was running his tavern as a house of private entertainment[39] and Josiah D. Burke of Loudoun County was operating the ordinary.[40] Burke, who lived at the ordinary,[41] was appointed Langley's postmaster on November 23, 1860.[41]

Georgetown lawyer Benjamin Mackall built a substantial home in Virginia and named it Langley. He owned the land upon which Billy Means operated a tavern, was the first president of the Falls Bridge Turnpike Company and became the postmaster at Langley in 1859. He voted to support the Ordinance of Secession in 1861. When Union troops occupied the Langley area, Mackall was taken from his home as a political prisoner and confined to the Capitol Prison in Washington City.

(Douglass Sorrel Mackall III)

This is the fourth bridge that spanned the Potomac River near Little Falls (1812-1840). It was built as a chain bridge and was the second chain bridge at that site. It stood when the Falls Bridge Turnpike Company opened a road that led from the bridge to the Alexandria-Leesburg Turnpike at Dranes Tavern. Langley residents and Virginia farmers were dependent upon this bridge for access to and from Georgetown and Washington City.                    (Library of Congress)

# CHAPTER 4
## Langley, the Walters Family and Civil War

As a cluster of structures began to form around Langley Fork, war clouds were gathering in the distant horizon that would pit neighbor against neighbor. The atmosphere across the nation was highly emotional: there was little room for compromise. After Abraham Lincoln's Presidential victory in November of 1860, states with deep Southern sympathies began to leave the Union to form their own government, the Confederate States of America. The secessionist movement met heavy resistance in the commonwealth, particularly in Northern Virginia. Many of these citizens hoped the Union could be saved and various methods of reconciliation were proposed. At a State Convention held in Richmond, an Ordinance of Secession was adopted on April 17, 1861, but it was subject to the ratification of Virginia's voters the following month on May 23, 1861.

There were already strong differences of opinion among friends, neighbors and family members, but approving or disapproving the Ordinance of Secession brought these hostilities to a head. Violence, or at least some harassment and intimidation, at many of the precincts occurred throughout the commonwealth on May 23, to assure that citizens cast their vote the "correct way:" in other words, to support the Ordinance of Secession. This was a vote that was cast by voice and was recorded in writing; thus, how a person voted became a matter of public record. At the end of the day, Virginians voted overwhelmingly to ratify the Ordinance of Secession, but the outcome at three precincts in Fairfax County was to remain with the Union: these were Lydecker's, Accotink, and Lewinsville.[1] Those who lived in Langley voted at the Lewinsville precinct. George Walters did not approve ratifying the Ordinance of Secession. However, the vote of his father-in-law William Means, supported secession, but not that of one of his sons, William A. Means, whose voice vote sided with the Union.[2] Walters claimed that he encountered intimidation at the Lewinsville precinct and later said that "I went there and noticed two or three pistols lying on the table among the commissioners, and after I voted I didn't stay there long."[3] He also felt that his anti-secession vote brought on a lifelong bitter hatred by many of his neighbors who held a different point of view.

During darkness the morning after Virginia's ratification became official, Union troops crossed the Potomac and took positions along the river's shoreline from Alexandria to the Chain Bridge in order to better protect the District of Columbia. In July of 1861, when after three days of fighting, Confederate forces overran those of the Union at the Battle of First Manassas. Federal troops rushed back to the City of Washington and Confederate troops pushed forward to occupy Falls Church and strategic hilltops in the immediate area. The victors did not advance upon the City of Washington as many predicted, but held their new positions, threatening America's capital and nearby villages. Those who voted against ratification found the atmosphere in their community extremely hostile. Confederate troops stationed nearby often drove Union supporters from their homes, forcing many to flee for safety in the District of Columbia.

The vicinity around Langley was filled with Southern sympathizers. Many loyal to the Union simply abandoned their houses and fled the area in fear of their lives. Even though Confederate troops were encamped in the immediate area, Walters elected to remain at Langley with his family, and Burke, also a Union supporter, continued to run the ordinary. Many residents in Langley who did not support the Union cause, and Southern cavalry troops stationed nearby, made several unsuccessful attempts to force Walters from his residence and take him prisoner. At one point, for over a month, Walters avoided capture by hiding in tree tops, the nearby woods and under the floors of some of the outbuildings on his property. Food was left for him at various places during the night by his oldest child, Marietta, until the Federal troops arrived to occupy the area, forcing the Southern troops and local sympathizers to leave. Major Evan Morrison Woodward, of the Third Pennsylvania Reserve, described Walters' situation before the Federal Army arrived in his book *History of the Third Pennsylvania Reserve*:

> "Captain Richards, being sick, received permission to move to the house of Mr. Walters, a wealthy farmer, who resided near Langley. Mr. W. was a staunch Unionist, and having strenuously opposed the secession of his State, incurred the bitter hatred of his life-long neighbors who favored it. They not being able to drive him and his family from their home, the aid of rebel cavalry was invoked, who made several descents upon his house at night, in hopes of capturing him. Mr. W., however, having no idea of going to Richmond, sometimes concealed himself in tree-tops, and at others under the floor of the out buildings, and succeeded in eluding them. At last he was forced to take to the woods, where he remained concealed for over a month, eluding their constant search. During this time food was brought by his daughter, Marietta, a brave, handsome, young girl, who at night with cat-like stillness, passed their guards, and deposited at certain places in the woods, without even awakening their suspicion. At last the Reserves came, and the rebels, chagrined at missing their prize, fired a number of cannon shot at the house and left." [4]

General George McCall's Pennsylvania Reserves, a Federal division of about 12,000 troops, left Tenleytown in the District of Columbia, and crossed the Chain Bridge on October 9 and 10, 1861, to establish Camp Pierpont in the Langley area. This camp was named after Francis Harrison Pierpont, the governor of Virginia. Most of McCall's troops were spread out along the Georgetown-Leesburg Turnpike up to the area around Prospect Hill.[5] At the same time, General William Farrar ("Baldy") Smith's division of at least 13,000 troops,[6] already stationed near the Chain Bridge while constructing Forts Ethan Allan and Marcy, spread out to establish Camp Griffin.[7] For several days, the Falls Bridge Road and the Georgetown-Leesburg Turnpike were covered with wagons transporting camp equipment for both divisions. Many houses in the Langley/Lewinsville area were deserted or quickly emptied as residents with Southern views, who had not already left the area, now hurried elsewhere at the sight of the approaching Union Army. McCall made use of Walters' ordinary for his headquarters:

> "THE NEW POSITIONS OF THE TROOPS --- A drizzling rain has been falling all the day, and our troops have been engaged in the double duty of strengthening their new outposts and arranging for their personal comfort as well as they can. The Leesburg turnpike, from Chain Bridge to Langley's, has been crowded with Government wagons all day, yet with all the camp equipage transported, many of the troops must bivouac in the rain tonight.

From Langley's west to Lewinsville nearly all the dwellings are deserted. Those belonging to Union families have been so since the retreat from Bull Run, though now Mr. CARPENTER, Mr. Green, Mr. Crocker, and Mr. Gilbert, who have been several weeks in Washington, will return to their homes tomorrow. The advance of our troops has caused the rebel families to remove to Secessin. Among them are those of HENRY JENKINS, a Colonel in the rebel cavalry; Mr. Murr and Mr. Cook, formerly of the Navy, but now rebel officers. Their places are on the road between Langley's and Lewinsville. Mr. Mackall, who lived near by, has also disappeared; and the residence of the family of the late Commodore ap CATSBY JONES, near Prospect Hill, was also found deserted. A son of the Commodore, PATTERSON JONES, of the Navy, has remained loyal to his country. Another son, MARK JONES, is a rebel officer. DURHAM, a rebel who kept a tavern at Langley's, has left. Mr. BURKE, a Union man who has a similar establishment at the same point, has been able to remain at his place throughout the difficulties. Mr. Smoot's dwelling, west of Langley's, until recently inhabited, was found without a tenant, and Gen. SMITH has located his head-quarters there. Gen. HANCOCK is at Dr. Mackall's, from which GRIFFIN'S Battery did such excellent service in the recent reconnaissance. The First Pennsylvania head-quarters is at Cooks"....[8]

Smith relocated his headquarters to Salona, now under the ownership of Jacob Smoot a Southern sympathizer who vacated his property and fled with his family into Georgetown. The Vermont Brigade, a part of Camp Griffin, encamped on the Salona grounds surrounding Smith's headquarters. The Langley area was now occupied by two divisions of the Army of the Potomac and two brigadier-generals whose headquarters were less than a mile from each other:

"ADVANCE OF GEN. McCALL'S DIVISION --- Gen. McCALL'S Division left Tennellytown during the night crossed the Potomac, and to-day occupied Langley, five miles from the Chain Bridge. Both his and Gen. SMITH'S head-quarters are at Langley.

The latter's division occupies the position it took yesterday; his pickets, however, have been advanced further into Virginia.

There are no indications of the presence of the enemy excepting cavalry pickets, and military officers incline to the opinion that there are no rebels in considerable force on the whole line of our Grand Army, or within six miles of its entire front."[9]

The ordinary was still in operation, with Burke in charge, when the Federal troops arrived. Means remained loyal to the Southern cause and, realizing that it would be "better for his health," abandoned his tavern and departed the area. The reporter for the *New York Times* in writing an article on the previous page mentions a fleeing Rebel named Durham as the owner of the tavern. There is no mention anywhere of a Durham in the Langley area or Fairfax County at that time. Possibly that was the name given the reporter, but the fleeing citizen was probably Means. As would be expected, Union soldiers were not respectful of his property as an article that appeared in the *New York Times* on October 30, 1861, suggests:

"Here was a striking illustration of how close the dividing lines are, which this unhappy war has drawn. Two taverns stand on the two sides of the road, nearly opposite. The landlord of one was a Secessionist, and had to flee, leaving his place to be trod by the reckless soldiery. The other was a Union man, and is still plying his vocation as unmolested as in times of peace."[10]

It is not known where Means sat out the war. His family was sharply divided regarding allegiance to the Union or the Southern position as seen by his family's vote at Lewinsville for the Ordinance of Secession. His oldest son Lewis Means was an officer with the Confederate army[11] and another son, Lt. George F. Means, rode with the 6th Virginia Cavalry.[12] But his son Samuel Means, who was a Quaker and successful owner of a gristmill in Waterford, was driven from his home for embracing the Union cause. With the authorization of Secretary of War Edward Staunton, Samuel formed and commanded the Independent Loudoun Rangers, a cavalry unit of scouts and spies.[13]

Walters was fortunate to escape capture from the Secessionists before Federal troops occupied the area, but his neighbor Benjamin Mackall who publicly supported the Ordinance of Secession at the Lewinsville precinct was not as lucky. Unlike those who continued to be loyal to the Southern cause and fled the area with the approach of the Federal Army, Mackall remained on his premises at the Mansion House of Langley. While inside his home, Mackall was arrested and taken to the Capitol Prison in the District of Columbia. Rather than being confined as a military prisoner, Mackall was considered a political prisoner who was suspected of giving information to the enemy. At the time of his arrest, his son William, a graduate of West Point, was a lieutenant-colonel in the Confederate Adjutant-General's Department serving under General Albert Sidney Johnson (he was promoted to general in the spring of 1862).[14] Mackall was not kept in prison for a lengthy period of time, but the Union was cautious. It did not want any information that Mackall might obtain at Langley to be relayed to his son. Thus, after his release he was restricted from going back to Virginia or communicating with any of its citizens and, so, he again took up residency in Georgetown.[15]

Soon after McCall established his headquarters in the ordinary, he called upon troops of the Brandywine Guards, Company A, First Pennsylvania Reserves, to serve as his body guard. Captain Mott Hooton, who received McCall's note asking for such support, replied in the affirmative. On October 19, 1861, Hooton wrote an informative letter home discussing the request. In writing, Hooton mentioned Walters' Grove, used the word tavern in describing the ordinary, and said that McCall granted permission for two unwell soldiers to stay at his headquarters:

> "We were marched to a field, where we formed in line of battle. I believe there was an attack expected, for the Generals were on an eminence where they planted some cannon, but as the enemy did not come we broke ranks and pitched our tents. Whilst we were in line an Orderly rode up and handed me a note, written in pencil. I opened it and found it from Gen. McCall, inquiring whether or not the Brandywine Guards, Company A, would act as his body guard, and requesting me to return an answer at the foot of the note, by the bearer. I replied that the Brandywine Guards would be happy to act as Gen. McCall's Body Guard.
>
> We pitched our tents and awaited further orders. Some time in the day Col. R. (Roberts) sent for me and gave me an order from the General that we were to report at 7 o'clock the next morning at his Head Quarters. Accordingly, this morning we got up bright and early, struck our tents, got breakfast, and marched down to the Colonel's quarters, who made a speech, telling us to behave ourselves, and keep up the dignity of the Regiment. He finished, we presented arms. He uncovered and bowed low. I dropped my sword to a salute. We then shouldered arms and marched off.

We reported to the General three minutes before the time. I inquired of the General what my duties were. He told me I was to guard his quarters and move whenever he moved. We have a delightful location in a beautiful grove of the finest forest trees, on a knoll just back of the tavern, which is his Excellencies' quarters.

Cheney Neilds and one of our men is not very well, and as we had no place to put them, I asked Dilwyn Parker to try and get them a room in the General's house; so Parker asked the General about it. He said that they could come and that Parker should fix a place for them, and his own cook should send them their meals...."[16]

On December 19, 1861, McCall received information that Confederate pickets had advanced to within four or five miles of the Federal line and had captured two Union men, threatened others, plundered the countryside, and stationed cavalry patrols at Dranesville. The tiny village was important to occupy because it was located where two turnpikes intersected: the Alexandria-Leesburg Turnpike and the Georgetown-Leesburg Turnpike. McCall ordered General Edward Ord's brigade to Dranesville for the purpose of capturing the Confederate forces there and, at the same time, bring back forage collected from farms owned by secessionists in the area. Ord left Camp Pierpont at 6:00 a.m. on December 20. His brigade, which consisted of four Pennsylvania Reserve regiments, was accompanied by Colonel Thomas Kane's First Rifles (Pennsylvania Reserves) from General George G. Meade's brigade; Captain Hezekiah Easton's battery consisting of four cannon; and two squadrons of cavalry. McCall also instructed General John F. Reynolds to take his First Brigade to Difficult Run where he was to wait and "support Ord in the event of his meeting a force stronger than his own."[17] That same morning, Confederate General Joseph E. Johnson, stationed at Centreville, ordered General J.E.B. Stuart to escort a foraging expedition north into Loudoun County. The foragers and wagons were guarded by four infantry regiments, 150 cavalry, and an artillery battery. The Confederate and Union expeditions stumbled into each other at Dranesville and a battle ensued between the two forces that lasted nearly two hours. At some point Reynolds was ordered forward to join the fight, but the First Brigade arrived too late to be of any assistance. When it was over, victory was claimed by the Union Army. The Union loss was seven killed and 61 wounded.[18] McCall's foragers brought back 16 wagons loaded with hay and 22 filled with corn.[19] General J.E.B. Stuart reported that the Confederates suffered 43 killed, 143 wounded, and eight missing.[20]

As winter arrived the life of a soldier became a harsh reality. Camp life was miserable and troops deserted from both sides. Some of the men were able to keep warm by building what was known as under-ground houses. Woodward wrote that "winter quarters consisted of walls of from four to six logs high, with wedge-tents placed above them. Floors of boards or logs were put down, shelves put up, and small sheet-iron stoves put in. From four to six soldiers generally bunked together, according to their liking...."[21] A soldier's daily life was fairly routine; it consisted of such things as picket duty, drilling, dress parades, inspections and foraging expeditions. As the winter became more severe, the mud was so deep that dress parades could not be held and the horses struggled to get through it. The food was inadequate, consisting mainly of hard tack and salt pork. Living in such cramped quarters was a breeding ground for sickness and disease. Troops at both Camps Pierpont and Griffin suffered from fever, pneumonia, diarrhea, typhoid fever, measles, diphtheria, cholera and mumps. Many of the vacated homes in the area, such as

Mackall's Mansion House and Benvenue, were turned into hospitals. The mortality rate was high. Sadly, many died without ever facing the enemy in battle. Woodward continued:

> "On the 27th, Private Peter W. Wittee, Company C, who died in the regimental hospital, was buried at Langley, with military honors, and the body of Private Joseph R. Barr, Company K, was sent to Philadelphia in charge of Lieutenant Donaghy. About the same time, Private Adam Martz, Company G, was buried at Langley, and the body of Lieutenant John Connally, Company G, was sent to Germantown in charge of Lieutenant Roberts. Orderly Sergeant Francis C. Harrison was elected Second Lieutenant, to fill the vacancy occasioned by the death of Lieutenant Connally...."[22]

> On the 3d of February, Private James Rose, Company C, died in camp and his comrades sent his body home. On the 27th Orderly Sergeant Sebastian Eckle, Company A, was elected Second Lieutenant in place of Lieutenant J. A. Clous, who resigned on account of ill health. On the 28th, Private George W. Morris, Company C, died, and Chaplain William H. Leake resigned on account of failing health, and the Reverend George H. Frear, of Reading, was appointed in his place...."[23]

The divisions of McCall and Smith occupied the Langley/Lewinsville area for six months. As spring approached Major General George McClellan, general-in-chief of the Union Army, was eager to undertake his Peninsula Campaign, in an attempt to capture Richmond. On March 10, 1862, both divisions "pulled up stakes" and departed the area. Various regiments, as part of the Defenses of Washington, were garrisoned at Forts Marcy and Ethan Allan to guard the Chain Bridge, but no single regiment remained for any length of time. For instance, the 118th New York Volunteer Regiment was at the Chain Bridge area a few weeks during October of 1862 and the 24th New Jersey Volunteer Infantry Regiment guarded the bridge from September 1, 1862 to April 1, 1862.

Burke continued with the ordinary operations until December of 1862. At that time he took leave of the Langley area and followed the 28th New Jersey Regiment down to Fredericksburg as part of a sutler's caravan. The sutler, who is a person who follows an army and sells provisions to the soldiers, resigned while at Falmouth, Virginia, in March of 1863, and Burke was selected by the officers of the 28th New Jersey Regiment to take over his position.[24] Burke only held this position for a short period because the 28th New Jersey was mustered out on July 6, 1863. He arrived back at Langley and, once again, began operating a house of public entertainment out of the ordinary. Because of wartime regulations he had difficulty in getting many of the necessary items to fulfill the needs of the Federal soldiers garrisoned nearby. Captain E. Young who was stationed at Fort Ethan Allen wrote to Colonel Henry Horatio Wells, Provost Marshall for Defenses South of the Potomac on October 1, 1863 requesting that Union requirements be lifted so that Burke would be able to provide goods suitable to sell to the troops:

> "Colonel: I have the honor to send enclosed my usual report for the last five days. Josiah Burke of Langley keeps a public house there and has always been accustomed to sell tobacco and various other articles usually sold by sutlers. Under the operation of Special Order: No. 4, he is not permitted to bring across the River any goods for sale. He is the most prominent loyal man in the region and if the provisions of the order could be relaxed in his case, I feel sure the privilege would not be abused."[25]

The Langley area was not occupied, but continued to be under Union control after the brigades of McCall and Smith left for the Peninsula Campaign. But many of the troops stationed at the two forts were often taken ill. A few were brought to Langley and the attic and one bedroom at the ordinary were used as a hospital. Some of the infirmed soldiers left their names on the bedroom or attic walls. In the spring of 1980, Lorraine Holdsworth, owner of the private residence that came to be known as the Langley Ordinary, removed wallpaper from a second floor bedroom and discovered the signatures. A few of the readable names included the following:

"Joseph A. Rogers. Co C (or G) N.Y. Regt. Jan. 14th 1863
Samuel G. Welch. C.O.B. 24th Regt. New Jersey Vols.
John O'Branner. Co. C ? 52
Henry A Sothard. ? 118th Regt.
James B. Rogers
A. Murray. 118th Regt. N.Y. Vol.
John ? Co. B. 112th Reg. Capt. G.W.? commanding
Don Picket. Dec. 26th 1862.
Capt. Natl. Wood. C. Buel Col. Com.
C. H. Groff. Co F (T or J) 11th Reg't.
S. Eneca T. Crossman. 118th Regt. Co.? N.Y.S.V.
Cl. (?) Behan. 169 Reg. Co. B. NYSV.
Norris. Co. E. 118th Reg. N.Y. State Volunteers.
William Getty."[26]

The fighting officially came to a close in Virginia with the surrender of Confederate General Robert E. Lee at Appomattox Court House on April 9, 1865. Like so many throughout the war-ravaged nation, the home-coming was challenging for residents in Langley as they picked up their broken lives and faced another challenge: Reconstruction and the struggle for survival.

Virginia's Ordinance of Secession was subject to voter approval through a referendum held on May 23, 1861. It was clear that Virginia would secede, but voter intimidation by a few secessionists took place to make certain that Virginians voted its passage. This *Harper's Weekly* cartoon suggests that voters, such as George Walters, encountered difficulties at the polls.   (*Harper's Weekly*)

General William Whann Mackall graduated from the United States Military Academy in 1837. At the start of the Civil War he was appointed a lieutenant colonel in the Confederate Army serving on the staff of General Albert Sidney Johnson. He was promoted to brigadier general in April, 1862. After the war, he returned to Langley and began a new life as a land speculator and farmer. He died in 1891, and is buried in the Lewinsville Cemetery.

(John T. Griffith)

The top 2005 photograph shows the structure built by George Walters in 1856 at the Langley Fork to serve as a drover's rest. Over the years it became known as the Langley Ordinary. The lower picture is General George A. McCall, the commander of the Pennsylvania Reserves. McCall used the ordinary as his headquarters during the Federal occupation of Langley during the winter of 1861/1862.                    (Top: Carole Herrick:  Lower: Library of Congress)

The above drawing shows the Pennsylvania Reserves at Langley Fork. Those on horses are turning onto the Falls Bridge Road; the ordinary is in the background to the right. The tavern is to the left and the toll house on the Georgetown-Leesburg Turnpike is in the distance. The bottom wood engraving depicts the guard house at Langley with Rebel prisoners.

(Top: Library of Congress)     (Bottom: Frank Leslies Illustrated Newspaper February 1, 1862)

General Edward Ord (top), commander of the 3$^{rd}$ Pennsylvania Reserves, led the attack against Confederate forces under the command of General J.E.B. Stuart (lower) at Dranesville.
(Both: Library of Congress)

Langley's Methodist Episcopal Church South was constructed in 1858. It also served as a hospital during the Civil War. In 1893 the Methodists erected a new church near the old structure. The original church building was converted into a residence for the Douglass Sorrell Mackall family and named Kirkwood. The above photograph of Kirkwood was taken in 1918 by J. Harry Shannon, a writer for the *Washington Star*, known as The Rambler.

(Fairfax County Public Library Archival Division)

Douglass Sorrell Mackall, the son of General William Whann Mackall, sold Hickory Hill to Susan Speer in 1916. In the later part of the nineteenth century Mackall, a practicing attorney and real estate speculator through the Langley Land Company, converted the original Langley Methodist Church into a residence for his family.

(Douglass Sorrel Mackall III)

# CHAPTER 5
## Hickory Hill

As four years of hostilities came to a close, citizens across the war-torn nation had to pick up their lives and deal with the problems of peacetime living. As a Quaker, George Walters did not join the military fighting forces. He remained at Langley overseeing his farm operations, witnessing continual injury to his property, and dealing with a loss of revenue from his drover's rest/ordinary. His situation was better than many of his neighbors who fled during the hostilities, only to return unprepared for the severity of the destruction to their property. Reconstruction was difficult in Langley, as it was throughout the commonwealth: animosities amongst neighbors still lingered. The pre-war sentiments were slow to change and neighbors found themselves not only struggling with rebuilding, but also struggling to cope with each other as they strived to piece their broken lives back together.

As commerce resumed along the war-ravaged Georgetown-Leesburg Turnpike, Means returned to resume his tavern operations. On November 28, 1865, he was again appointed as Langley's postmaster: this was a position he held until March 28, 1867. At that time the operations at Langley's post office briefly ceased until Burke took over the position again on April 12, 1867. Burke only served in this capacity until December 15, 1867.[1] After that, he moved into the District of Columbia where he became a police officer.[2] By now George and Mary Walters were raising seven children: Marietta, Sarah, James, George Jr., Alexander, Mary, and Ulysses. The older boys assisted with the farm operations, giving their father some freedom to take on additional responsibilities regarding local and county affairs. Before the war came to a close, Walters began serving during October of 1864 as a Justice of the Peace for Fairfax County, a position he held for several years.[3] The Georgetown-Leesburg Turnpike was in deplorable condition due to military usage and, of course, during the war years, tolls had not been collected. After the war a new board of directors was formed and Walters was appointed to this board on September 28, 1865.[4] Tolls were again collected. By 1867 the fee at Langley was 15 cents.[5] Possibly due to the unpleasant experience he encountered when casting his vote not to ratify the Ordinance of Secession, Walters briefly took on the job of Commissioner of Elections at the Lewinsville Precinct beginning on May 26, 1864.[6]

According to Rosemary (Walters) Goodman, a third generation Walters' family member by marriage, the home of George Walters was destroyed by a fire in 1862: it started when a servant tipped over a lighted candle. In a 1963 letter written to Ethel Kennedy (a later occupant of Hickory Hill), Goodman wrote that it was a windy night. The ground was covered with snow and a very young George Walters, Jr., ran barefoot through it shouting for help, but by the time assistance arrived, it was too late; the house had burned to the ground.[7] Goodman goes on to suggest that another house which Walters named Hickory Hill was completed in 1864 and constructed on the foundations of the earlier house that burned.[8] There is no account of this incident by any soldier of the Pennsylvania Reserves, those stationed at Camp Griffin, other regiments that later guarded Chain Bridge or troops that occupied the ordinary. If a fire occurred during the war, as suggested, there would have been Federal soldiers encamped nearby and help would have quickly arrived.

The Fairfax County Land Tax Books show that the assessed value of Walters' acreage at Langley decreased substantially in 1864, rather than showing an increase that would have resulted had a house the size of Hickory Hill been erected. The tax assessments in 1859, 1860, 1861, and 1863 (county records do not show assessed values in 1862) list the value of Walters land and buildings at a constant $5425, but in 1864, the assessment decreased by $500 to $4925.[9] The 1864 reduction was probably due to Walters appealing to the Fairfax County tax commissioners in February of 1865 to reduce his tax assessments at Langley for the years 1862, 1863, and 1864 due to the war. In his appeal, there is no mention of a fire:

> "I Geo. F. M. Walters respectively represent that I am owner of certain tracts of land in said County, a portion of which is entirely outside of the Federal lines, the remainder within the lines a part of the time. I have not had sufficient protection to enable me, or any one for me, to pursue the ordinary course of farming upon the said farm during the past four years.
>
> I do solemnly swear that I have never voluntarily given aid, comfort, or information to the enemies of the United States by act or deed.
>
> I, therefore, ask the taxes assessed against me for the years 1862, 1863, and 1864, be remitted."[10]

If there was a fire, as Goodman suggests, it would have taken place in 1867 because Walters' tax assessment on the Langley property was lowered another $500 in 1868 to $4424.63 and included $200 for alterations during the preceding year. However, two years later, in 1870, the land and property assessment substantially increased to $11,424.63, indicating that sizeable improvements were added to his land that would have included at least two new sizeable structures: a very large bank barn and a magnificent dwelling house built by Walters that he named Hickory Hill.[11]

There are two maps that include a residence for Walters on the Falls Bridge Road prior to 1870. The first is titled "Surveys for Military Defenses Map of North Eastern Virginia and Vicinity of Washington" and was completed under the direction of the Bureau of Topographical Engineers on August 1, 1862. It is a second edition of what is known as the "McDowell Map of January 1, 1862," and is far denser than the previous version. Numerous structures in the Langley area are clearly indicated on the second edition and a spot is shown along the Falls Bridge Road where a dwelling for Walters would have been.[12] "A Detailed Map of Part of Virginia from Alexandria to the Potomac River above Washington, D. C.," produced by the United States Army Corps of Engineers is dated 186_ by the Library of Congress. This map includes a dwelling on the Lewinsville Road (the Falls Bridge Road) labeled Walters. The Freedman's Village in Arlington is also shown on this map.[13] Freedman's Village was established in May of 1863. Even though the year this map was produced is uncertain, it does provide evidence that Walters had a house along the Falls Bridge Road in 1863. Because of the increased land and property assessment in 1870, the house depicted on the two maps is undoubtedly the earlier farmhouse; thus, giving support for Goodman's story that Hickory Hill was built on the site, or possibly the foundation, of an earlier house.

On October 6, 1866, through a deed of trust with William Cassin a Georgetown lawyer, John and Mary Trammel purchased ten acres from Walters for $5000 that included the ordinary.[14] Trammel collateralized his house in Georgetown in order to secure his debt to Walters for this purchase.[15] The terms of the deed stated that if he defaulted on the debt, the Langley property could then be put up for public sale and sold to the highest bidder.[16] Trammel was unable to keep up with the payments and defaulted on the loan.[17] Walters regained the property, and on February 1, 1870, he reconveyed it to Rosanna St. Clair, a widow who lived in Georgetown and sold furniture.[18] St. Clair also signed a deed of trust with Cassin as trustee to secure the loan through two promissory notes. The terms of the deed were the same as those for Trammel: if she defaulted on the payments, the property could be sold at a public auction.[19] Like Trammel, she was unable to make the payments, and the auction took place on April 7, 1874. Walters, being the highest bidder, bought back the ten acre ordinary property for $2400.[20]

Throughout the Trammel and St. Clair ownership, the ten acres remained on the tax records as belonging to Walters and the use of the ordinary under their ownership cannot be determined. Both Trammel and St. Clair resided in the District of Columbia and neither of them appeared to have ever lived in the building or was issued a license to operate an ordinary, tavern, drovers rest or house of entertainment. It is possible that the building remained vacant during their ownership. However, Goodman wrote that the Walters family moved into the ordinary after the fire. If this happened it would have been during the Trammel tenure.

Unfortunately, records have not been found (at least at this point) to verify Goodman's account regarding a fire. This is not to claim that there was not a fire, but whether it occurred in 1862, as she suggests, is questionable. Many Virginia records, such as insurance claims, were lost or destroyed during the war or in the early days of Reconstruction. Whatever the case, the evidence indicates that a new home was completed for the Walters family by 1870. The older, much smaller, farmhouse was either destroyed by a fire ca.1862-1867 or taken down ca.1867, as evidenced by the 1868 Fairfax County Land Tax Records. The family needed a place to live during the time of construction. The ordinary was the logical location. Possibly Trammel allowed the Walters family to reside there while the new house was being built in lieu of the payments he was unable to meet on the loan he had on the property.

Besides having a reputation as an exceptional farmer, Walters was considered to be a highly skilled carpenter. He built Hickory Hill atop a low hill on the east side of the Falls Bridge Road and completed it in late 1869 or early 1870. Hickory Hill was a large red brick residence with a slate mansard roof. This was a French roofing style that was just becoming fashionable in the United States. The driveway was built in a semi-circle; thus, there were two entrances from the Falls Bridge Road. According to Goodman, all of the bricks, doors, window frames, and molding were made on the property. She briefly described the house in her letter to Kennedy:

"All the bricks were handmade from clay dug on the property, and there must have been thousands of them. George F. M. Walters, Sr., was a master carpenter. Every door, window-frame, and molding was handmade on the place. He employed a large force of carpenters and, according to his grandson who has the account book for the construction of Hickory Hill, his carpenters made fifty cents per day. The house originally had a slate mansard roof. He named it 'Hickory Hill.'"[21]

Shortly after its completion, the first of many social events was held at Hickory Hill on June 16, 1870. This was the wedding of the Walters' oldest daughter Marietta to George Curley, of Maryland.[22] Marietta was the daughter that brought Walters food while he was hiding from his neighbors and Confederate troops during the very early stages of the war, and who the Federal soldiers found so gracious. Unfortunately, the joyous event was short lived. Marietta died in Baltimore on April 10, 1871, less than one year after her marriage. She was 24 years of age.[23]

In 1871, Congress authorized a United States Southern Claims Commission which considered the applications of at least 200 residents from Fairfax County.[24] It was only natural that many Union supporters, who lived in states that seceded, sought compensation from the Federal government for property they claimed was destroyed or taken by the Federal troops. George Walters and his older brother, William, filed with the Southern Claims Commission. William filed Claim Number 1730 on May 29, 1871, seeking $727 for damages to his property near Wolf Den Run. He had voted against the Ordinance of Secession at Lydecker's and, at one point, was a scout for General Winfield Hancock. He was allowed $235.[25] George Walters filed Claim Number 506 requesting $6000. His testimony, along with that of three others, was not heard in Washington by the commissioners, but was considered by appointed persons in Richmond on June 13, 1871. This unusual action occurred because the Southern Claims Commissioners "decided that their jurisdiction does not extend to claims for rent or occupation of buildings and grounds for military purposes, and that they are not empowered to report to Congress on the merits of any such claims."[26] The claim of George F. M. Walters was heard the following day, but his request was only partially granted; he was awarded $1524.75.[27]

Reconstruction brought some change to Langley. Walters Grove continued as the place to hold large gatherings, but events, such as ice cream socials and strawberry festivals that highlighted the summer were usually held on church grounds. The temperance movement remained strong. The Methodists constructed a Temperance Hall on the north side of the Georgetown-Leesburg Turnpike and temperance gatherings were once again held in Walters Grove.[28] In 1866, Langley's second house of worship, the St. John's Episcopal Church was founded and the initial services were held in the existing Methodist Church or in private homes.[29] The Episcopalians eventually raised enough money to build a small Gothic church on the south side of the Georgetown-Leesburg Turnpike on land given by Author Taylor and consecrated in 1877.[30] The black population, which worshipped at the Methodist Church, began meeting in the home of Robert Gunnell, a former slave freed by Benjamin Mackall in 1856.[31] Gunnell acquired 6.5 acres adjoining the Mackall Farm at Langley Fork before the war began. It was on a portion of this property that black Methodists built a two-story building fronting the Georgetown-Leesburg Turnpike sometime during the 1870s. This served the blacks in the

Langley area as both a church and a school until construction began on the same site for Gunnell's Chapel in 1899.[32] White Methodists eventually decided to construct a new church. A wooden white clapboard structure was built very near the original building and called the Langley Methodist Church. It had stained glass windows, an asymmetrical bell tower and wooden buttresses built against the side walls: the new church was completed in 1893.[33] Douglass Sorrell Mackall, a son of General William Mackall, then converted the original Methodist church building into a residence for his family.[34]

Besides the changes that were taking place in the way of new buildings, there were also improvements made to existing structures. For instance, in 1889 Walters decided to completely renovate the ordinary, (known then as Langley Flats). When finished, it was occupied by one of his sons George Walters, Jr. and his wife Katherine.[35] The toll house still remained, between Gunnell's Chapel and the four acres occupied by James Walters, even though tolls were not collected. A Confederate cavalry veteran named Braden Hummer decided to give up farming to open a general store. He signed a five year lease with Priscilla Reid on February 6, 1889, to rent the toll house property at $3 a month. The lease said that he "shall have the right to move, remodel, and reconstruct the buildings on said premises, and shall have the right and privilege of erecting any and all buildings and improvements…which he may desire."[36] The terms of the lease also stated that when the lease ended, Hummer had the right to take the buildings with him or that Reid could purchase them.[37] Hummer remodeled the toll house structure and, along with his wife Willella, opened a general store later that same year. The *Fairfax Herald* reported on May 24, 1889:

> "Mr. B. E. Hummer has completed his store and dwelling house. It is quite an improvement to the village. His new stand is by far preferable to the old one."[38]

Even though Langley was adjacent to the District of Columbia, the area continued as a rural agricultural community where farmers sowed oats, grew corn, planted potatoes, harvested hay, slaughtered pigs and milked dairy cows. Drovers constantly herded their cattle, sheep, pigs, or flocks of turkeys and geese through the village on their way to the Georgetown markets. An example of the continued agrarian atmosphere is apparent in the following 1899 advertisement in the *Alexandria Gazette* that was taken out by George F. M. Walters, Jr., a cattle dealer:

# "COWS

PUBLIC AUCTION OF FRESH COWS.
I will sell at public auction on MONDAY, OC-
TOBER THIRTIETH, AT ELEVEN O'CLOCK A.M.,
at Langley, Va. (three miles from Chain Bridge), a
carload of Fresh Cows from the Valley of Virginia.
GEORGE F. WALTERS."[39]

George Franklin Means Walters died at Hickory Hill on February 23, 1890, at the age of 75. He was buried in the Lewinsville Cemetery adjacent to the Lewinsville Presbyterian Church.[40] Walters left a life interest in his entire estate, real and personal, to his wife Mary, but upon her death everything was to be equally divided among their remaining six children: George, Alexander, James, Ulysses, Sarah, and Mary. Walters' will stated that three of his sons could keep the property they already held, but their ownership came with limitations: James, George, and Alexander had property that was included in the estate left to Mary. Walters had outstanding debts. Before his death, each of the three sons had been offered the option of purchasing the parcel of land awarded to him that was part of the estate. It was a verbal agreement that each son agreed to accept: it was understood that James would pay $500 for his four acres along the Georgetown-Leesburg Turnpike, George, Jr. would offer $4000 for his ten acres that included Langley Flats (the ordinary), and Alexander would give $4000 for his 40 acres along the Georgetown-Leesburg Turnpike. The youngest son, Ulysses and his wife, Hattie, were living at Hickory Hill and obligated to pay rent to Mary and farm the land to help eliminate the debt. Furthermore, Alexander was married to Irma Storm. The couple held an 83 acre parcel near Lewinsville that had been part of John Storm's farm. The property was encumbered by $450. They were expected to sell it to Mary at a price of $2000 and she would assume the encumbrance.[41]

The last will and testament of George F. M. Walters was made on February 22, 1890, the day before he died. It was witnessed by Lewis Means.[42] Mary was named the executor, but the six children questioned her entitlements and the will was immediately probated. Agreement was reached between the various parties on May 19, 1890. George, James, and Alexander were not in a position to pay cash for their "inheritance," but each gave signed notes to the estate that were secured by a deed of trust for the deferred payments. Ulysses and his wife were allowed to continue residency at Hickory Hill on a year to year rental basis, paying Mary $500 annually. It was only the four sons that incurred financial pain with Walters' passing. The second daughter Sarah, the wife of Samuel Hutson, had purchased the adjoining 52 acre Johnson property in 1878[43] and the youngest daughter, Mary, was allowed to remain living in the house with her mother until she later married Frank Hough.[44]

Around the time of Walters' death, discussions had started regarding building an electrified railroad that would run from Rosslyn to Great Falls Park and connect with Washington, D.C. via the Aqueduct Bridge.[45] Residents in Langley, as were those in Lincolnville (renamed Chesterbrook ca.1897) and Lewinsville, were excited about such a venture. The rail line would provide an easier and faster way for farmers to get their products to market, a simpler way to commute to and from the District of Columbia, and the possibility of increased commerce to the village where the station was placed. Residents in Langley were hopeful that the tracks for the Great Falls and Old Dominion Railroad would be laid through, or near, their village. After the necessary land purchases, the rails were laid through fields and orchards, completely bypassing Langley. A planned community named Ingleside began to develop where the tracks crossed the Falls Bridge Road (Chain Bridge Road)[46] and, so, the stop at that location was called Ingleside. The trolley first began to carry passengers to and from Great Falls Park on July 4, 1906.[47] By July of 1910 the Ingleside stop became known as McLean. It was renamed for John R. McLean, one of the organizers of the railroad and owner of the *Washington Post* newspaper.[48] The following year, area post offices at Lewinsville and Langley were discontinued and consolidated into the McLean Post Office located inside Storm's General Store at the rail stop.[49] The hub of area activity now centered around Storm's General Store and the McLean stop. Chesterbrook continued with its post office, eventually operating out of Stalcup's General Store until being taken over by the Falls Church Post Office. In effect, the arrival of the Great Falls and Old Dominion Railroad was a death sentence for the three villages. Lewinsville, Langley, and later Chesterbrook, gradually faded away to become names of the past as they were absorbed by the new community of McLean.

George F. M. Walters, Jr., died tragically at the age of 38 before the trolley line opened. He was accidentally run over by a train engine in Alexandria's Southern Railway Yard in the late evening of December 8, 1905. Walters was a cattle dealer who had come to Alexandria to oversee the unloading of a carload of dairy cows. After paying the freight charges at the depot office, he was struck by an engine while on his way back to the cows. He was rushed to the hospital in Alexandria where he died a short time later. An article in the *Fairfax Herald* described the horrific event:

> "Mr. Geo. F. Walters, a well known resident of the Langley neighborhood was accidentally killed at the depot in Alexandria last Thursday night. The Gazette gives the following account of the unfortunate affair:
>
> George F. Walters, a cattle dealer of Langley Fairfax county, was run over by a light engine in the Southern Railway yard in this city between 11 and 12 o'clock Thursday night and so seriously injured that he died soon after being removed to the Alexandria Hospital. The unfortunate man leaves a widow and several small children.
>
> Mr. Walters had come to Alexandria in charge of a carload of cattle and had proceeded to the office in the yard for the purpose of settling the freight charges. He was on his way back when a light engine that had arrived from Washington struck and ran over him, severing his right arm and inflicting internal injuries. The engineer saw Mr. Walters' satchel roll on an opposite track, and, supposing something had fallen from the locomotive, stopped it, when he discovered that it had run over Mr. Walters. He was picked up and taken to the hospital.
>
> Dr. O'Brian was called to attend the man at 11:00 o'clock, and with Dr. Jones proceeded to the hospital at once where they found Walters in a most deplorable condition. His skull was crushed front and back and his right arm badly mangled. The doctors amputated the mangled arm, dressed the wounds on his head and did all in their power for the relief of the unfortunate man, but to no avail, and soon thereafter, as stated above, he expired.
>
> The deceased had $1,500 in his satchel when killed. Master Mechanic W. F. Kaderly was one of the first who went to his assistance. The accident occurred within a few yards of the spot where Mordecai Hurst was recently run over and killed. The remains were taken to Lewinsville for internment."[50]

As was his father, Walters was interned in the Lewinsville Cemetery. His wife, Katherine, was able to continue living at the ordinary with their seven children. Less than a year later, tragedy struck Katherine once again when her 18 year old son William accidentally drowned in the Potomac River. William was swimming about a mile above the Aqueduct Bridge with six other friends on the afternoon of September 8, 1906, when strong currents swept him under the surface of the water. His body was later found near the bridge. William Walters was buried in the Lewinsville Cemetery beside the grave of his father. The *Evening Star* reported the unfortunate event the following day:

"William H. Walters, eighteen years old, of Langley, Va., was drowned in the Potomac river off Forty-foot rock, on the Virginia shore, a mile above the Aqueduct bridge, about 3 o'clock yesterday afternoon. The efforts of the six persons who had been with him and of the crew of the police launch Major Sylvester failed to recover the body.

The young man graduated from the Western High School last spring, and is said to have been a good student. He was a substitute on the base ball team, and was popular among the boys at the school. He lived with his mother in Langley, Va., and through police headquarters she was notified last night of the drowning. The boy, it is stated, worked for the telephone company in this city, but this could not be confirmed last night....

The place where the party were swimming, and where it is believed Walters was drowned, is one of the deepest holes in the river and the currents are very strong.

In their efforts to communicate with the relatives of the boy the police reached the residence of U. S. Walters at Langley, Va., by telephone, and it was stated he was an uncle of the boy, and that the boy's mother lived only a short distance away. Mr. Walters notified the mother. The dead boy's father is dead, it was stated."[51]

The grief the entire Walters family faced with two tragic deaths so close together was enormous. For Mary it was a son and a grandson; for Katherine it was her husband and a son. But there were other unfortunate incidents during this time-frame that required Mary's attention. Lightning struck the Hickory Hill property in 1906. Mary was awarded $30.43 by the Independent Mutual Fire Insurance Company, of Fairfax County for fire damage.[52] The following year the house was badly damaged by fire. Mary's insurance policy still remained with the Independent Mutual Fire Insurance Company whose records show that in 1907 she had an unadjusted claim for $1100 for fire losses and her son Ulysses had a claim of $500.[53]

Mary outlived her husband by twenty years: she died at age 85 on January 23, 1910,[54] and was interned beside her husband in the Lewinsville Cemetery. In May of the previous year she was given a surprise 84th birthday party at Hickory Hill. The *Evening Star* included a descriptive account of the event on May 16, 1909:

"Tuesday, May 11, 1909, at her beautiful old home, Hickory Hill, Langley, Fairfax county, Va., Mrs. Mary A. Walters, wife of the late George F. M. Walters, was given a celebration in honor of her eighty-fourth birthday. The lovely old lady was taken completely by surprise, as she had forgotten the date, and when one family after the other came in and congratulated and presented her with flowers and presents she seemed mystified at first, but by the time she was seated at the dinner table as hostess to her many guests she realized it all.

Her guest of honor was her fond old friend, Mrs. R. A. Van Dyke, wife of the late Dr. Van Dyke of that county. Among those of her children and friends who were there to wish her many happy returns were Mr. and Mrs. J. W. Walters, Mr. and Mrs. Frank Pugh and son Harry, Mrs. A. B. Walters and her daughters, Mrs. Roland, Mrs. Alice Hutson, Mrs. Katie Walters, Mr. and Mrs. U. S. Walters, Miss K. Burr Walters, Miss Jennie Walters, Miss Pearl Walters, little Dorothy Walters, Messrs. Fenton, Robert, Douglas, and Master Milton Walters. Mr. and Mrs. Taylor, Mrs. L. Turner, Miss May Walters,

Mrs. Shafer, Miss Olive Shafer. Mr. and Mrs. U. S. Walters, who live at the old home with Mrs. Mary Walters, their mother, entertained and served all the guests in a most charming and hospitable manner and the day was a happy one to all."[55]

As per the will of her husband, Mary's estate was to be equally divided among their six children. By the time of Mary's death, however, there were only five children to divide the property: James, Alexander, Ulysses, Sarah Hutson, and Mary Hough. Animosities arose between the heirs regarding the division of the estate. Even though George F. M. Walters, Jr., was deceased, his family continued to live at the ordinary, and, as his widow, Katherine felt that her children and she were entitled to her husband's one-sixth share of the estate. There was also dissention between Alexander and Frank Hough, the husband of Sarah Walters, concerning a 1913 sale of Alexander's one-sixth portion to Hough.[56] An agreement was worked out that would settle the estate except for two parcels of real estate located in Langley: the 77 acre Hickory Hill property and the 20 acres purchased from Sarah and Samuel Randall in 1853. These two tracts became the subject of a partition suit among the heirs: the case of *James W. Walters, and complaints vs. Katherine H. Walters, and complaints*, was in litigation in the Circuit Court of Fairfax County beginning March 24, 1914. A settlement could not be reached amongst the heirs on how the property should be equally divided. Thus, Douglass Sorrell Mackall was appointed as a Special Commissioner of Sale in the chancery suit. He was given authorization to put Hickory Hill up for sale and to distribute the proceeds equally amongst the heirs.[57]

A journalist/photographer named J. Harry Shannon walked through Langley and passed by Hickory Hill in the summer of 1914.[58] His nom de plume was "The Rambler." Shannon wrote for the *Evening Star* newspaper from 1890 to 1895 and was a member of its editorial staff from 1900 to February 12, 1928. As he walked along his various routes, Shannon would spend time discussing the area with residents. His journeys turned into an oral history of the Greater Washington area: his articles and accompanying photographs were based upon these conversations. Because of the pending litigation, Ulysses had moved out of Hickory Hill and, so, it was vacant when Shannon walked by. However, he included a brief description of Hickory Hill in a story he later wrote:

> "...Soon after branching onto this road at Langley you see on the left a large red brick house with a mansard slate roof, situated on a low green hill, oak-shaded by venerable specimens of the forest monarch. The place is called Hickory Hill. This was the property of George F. M. Walters, and the old settlers out there remember him as one of the progressive and therefore prosperous farmers in that part of the country."[59]

After retracing his steps back to Langley on this same afternoon, Shannon stopped at the ordinary and engaged Katherine in conversation. In describing his visit there, "The Rambler" wrote the following:

> "...In the southwest angle of the Leesburg pike and the road to Salona an aged-looking house stands sheltered by oak and hickory trees. It was a picket post throughout the war. Sometime after the war the rooms were papered, and not so long ago it was concluded to repaper them. In removing the old paper the whitewashed walls were found to be written over with soldiers names, and many of these have been left exposed. You could spend half a day deciphering these names, some clearly written and some scrawled. At a glance

the Rambler read these: "Sergt. Frank Foster, Co. C., 27th Reg. C. Vols. On picket duty Nov. 3, 1862:' 'Andrew Land, Jr., Co. D 28th N. J. Vols.:' D. V. Okey, D 28th N. J. Vols:' 'Ambrose W. Hastings, New Haven.'

The lady living there told the Rambler that the house was at one time the headquarters of Gen. McCall, and she pointed to a wooden bracket by means of which a telegraph wire had been run into the house. The house was built as a Drovers' Rest by George F. M. Walters, the builder of Hickory Hill about 1856. It was taken possession of by troops early in 1861 and held until after the surrender of the Confederate armies. Then it had become a tavern and a store.

The lady said that she had heard that during the war a soldier had been murdered in a small room off the dining room and that a negro servant had died of smallpox in a room above the kitchen. She had lived there since 1890: Her name is Mrs. Catherine Walters, widow of George Walters, son of the builder of the house. She showed the Rambler through the big rooms. The house is heavily and stoutly built of hewn and mortised oak timbers and with broad open fireplaces.

On the north side of the pike, nearly opposite the Walter's house, is an old structure which was opened there as a tavern more than a century ago, but has not been used for that purpose a number of years...."[60]

Mackall was able to bring about the sale of Hickory Hill to the satisfaction of both the claimants and defendants: the 77 acre property was sold to Susan Speer on March 23, 1916, for $18,000.[61] The ordinary, which was not part of the suit, was later sold to Sallie Loving on September 18, 1919, for $7000.[62]

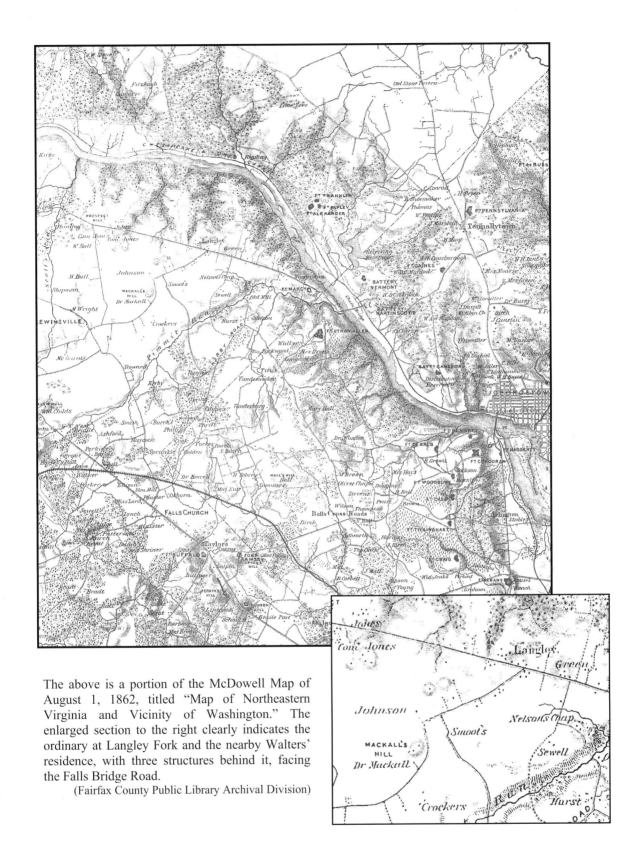

The above is a portion of the McDowell Map of August 1, 1862, titled "Map of Northeastern Virginia and Vicinity of Washington." The enlarged section to the right clearly indicates the ordinary at Langley Fork and the nearby Walters' residence, with three structures behind it, facing the Falls Bridge Road.

(Fairfax County Public Library Archival Division)

49

This is a section of the "Detailed Map of Part of Virginia to the Potomac River above Washington, D.C., 186_" as drawn by the Army Corps of Engineers. It clearly shows the Walters farmhouse, the grove and Langley Fork. What is labeled the Lewinsville Road is today's Chain Bridge Road. The Walters residence burned shortly after the Civil War and was replaced with a substantial structure named Hickory Hill ca.1870.

(Library of Congress)

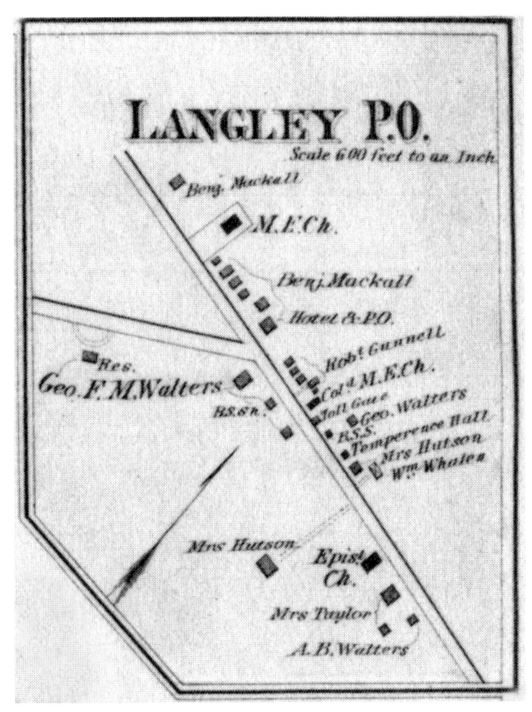

The above is an enlarged portion of the Langley community produced from plate 11 of 11 titled "Providence Dist. No 5" from Griffith M. Hopkins' 1879 *Atlas of Fifteen Miles Around Washington Including the Counties of Fairfax and Alexandria, Virginia*. The property of George Walters is clearly shown. The house is identified in the same location as the previous two maps, but the driveway is now a semi-circle, providing some credence that Hickory Hill was built after the Civil War on the site of a former farmhouse. The property labeled Mrs. Hutson belonged to the Walters second daughter Sarah, the wife of Samuel Hutson, and that of A.B. Walters was owned by their third son Alexander. (*The Cartography of Northern Virginia*)

51

This is a photograph of the stately red brick Hickory Hill mansion built by George Walters ca.1870. It was taken from an original oil painting that remains with Walters descendants. It shows the slate mansard roof, the cupola above it and the semi-circular driveway opening onto the Falls Bridge Road. A surrounding porch was added in the early 1920s by the James Speer family.

(The Dabbiere Family)

Harry Shannon took this photo of the ordinary as he rambled through Langley in 1917. Katherine Walters continued living there until it was sold to Sallie Loving in 1919.

(Connie and Mayo Stuntz)

# CHAPTER 6
## The Speer Residency

Susan Speer was the wife of Dr. James Pat Speer, a dentist who practiced in Washington, D. C. at the time of the Hickory Hill purchase. On February 25, 1916, Susan's husband submitted an offer to Douglass Sorrell Mackall, a Special Commissioner of Sales, to buy the 77 acre estate for $18,000. Speer's letter was written as follows:

"Dear Sir:

I hereby offer the sum of eighteen thousand dollars, ($18,000.00) for what is known as the Walters property, located on the East side of the road between Langley and McLean, and supposed to contain 77 acres of ground, improved by a brick dwelling, large barn, etc. The purchase price to be paid as follows:

Two thousand dollars ($2000.00) less the sum of $1000.00 now paid in connection with this offer, in cash, $5000.00 one (1) year, after date: $5000.00 two (2) years after date, and the balance $6000.00 three (3) years after date, said deferred payments to be evidenced by my notes, with interest at the rate of six (6) per centum per annum, payable semi-annually, and be secured by a vendor's lean, or deed of trust on the property sold, all of said notes being payable on or before maturity, and to be in such amounts as you may prefer, and as collateral to the payment of the first of said notes. I agree to deposit the real estate note for $5000.00 mentioned to you.

It is understood that cost of examination of title, all conveyancing, recording, internal revenue stamps and notary fees shall be at my expense; that this offer is subject to the approval of the Court, that the title shall be a good one free of all liens, and encumbrances, and taxes; that said notes shall be dated and adjustments of taxes, and insurance, shall be made to date of deed: the purchaser shall have full possession of said property upon compliance with the terms of sale; that should this offer be not approved by the Court or the title be not good the sum of $1000.00 now paid shall be refunded to me, whereupon all liability under this contract shall cease and determine: terms of sale to be complied with as soon as the Court shall approve this offer provided that such approval shall be obtained within sixty days from this date. Dated, Washington, D. C. February 25, 1916.

Yours truly,

J. P. Speer"[1]

Mackall thought that it was in the best interest of the combative Walters heirs to accept Speer's offer. With the consent of both parties he was given permission to proceed with the sale and to close it as quickly as possible. Less than a month after Speer submitted his letter to Mackall, Hickory Hill passed from the Walters family to that of the Speers for the sum of $18,000, which included a cash payment of $2000. A balance of $16,000 was incurred through a deed of trust for the remainder of the purchase price. The debt consisted of eight promissory notes that were to be paid in installments over a period of three years. Speer did not put his signature on the actual deed, but transferred the purchase of the property to his wife, who did sign it. Thus, the 77 acre Hickory Hill property was conveyed to Susan Virginia Speer by Special Commissioner of Sale Mackall on March 23, 1916, and she became the official owner of Hickory Hill.[2]

Speer learned his dental skills from his father, Spencer Hadley Speer. The elder Speer was a pioneer dentist who, after serving in Company F, 37th Virginia Cavalry Battalion, during the Civil War, practiced his profession from a horse-drawn buggy traveling throughout Russell County, Virginia.[3] It appears that, in the beginning, Speer was very successful in following the dental footsteps of his father, but unfortunately, he lacked morality when it came to family matters and did not seem to have any control over his personal life. James and Susan Speer were married in 1896[4] and before moving into Hickory Hill twenty years later, they had relocated at least seven times. After their marriage they resided in Smyth County, Virginia, for about two years; Russell County, Virginia, nearly three years: Washington County, Virginia, close to three years; back to Russell County for almost five years; Charlotte, North Carolina, only eleven months; Birmingham, Alabama, about three years; and the City of Washington where they lived eleven months before moving to Virginia's countryside in McLean.[5]

By the time they settled into Hickory Hill, the Speers had six children: Madeline, Ira, Lucile, Spencer, James, and Virginia.[7] Susan's life was difficult. But it was more than simply the challenging task of living in the country and raising their children: intoxicating liquor and adulterous behavior with other women dominated the life of her husband and his judgment was more than often clouded. This was the pre-prohibition era where liquor flowed freely and Speer enjoyed its consumption and all the pleasures that were associated with it. While living in Alabama, Speer was treated for alcoholism at a facility that offered the Keeley Cure. This was a pioneering four week series of injections and tonics known as the "Gold Cure" that treated alcoholism as a medical disease, rather than a social vice. The treatments apparently had little effect because Speer's drinking continued and his behavior became increasingly bizarre. On two occasions while at Hickory Hill, he sought help again through the Keeley Cure, but the treatments did not result in the sought after cure for his alcoholic problems.[8]

In spite of the various difficulties created by his excessive drinking, Speer's dental practice flourished. During his time at Hickory Hill, he had at least three offices in the City of Washington and one in Baltimore. Still he continued with his drinking and adulterous misconduct with other women. On September 13, 1921, the large bank barn on the property that was constructed by Walters was destroyed by fire.[9] Speer approached his wife requesting that she turn the Hickory Hill deed over to him. He insisted that it was necessary for her to do this in order for him to collect the insurance on the ruined barn. Susan declined. In a further effort to have the deed transferred over to him, Speer brought a woman friend that he had been seeing for some time out to Hickory Hill.[10] The pressure proved too much for Susan and she handed the deed over to her husband, who assured her that he would not record it, and even promised to return the deed to her after the insurance claim was paid. The transfer was never recorded, and he did not return the deed.

It was around this time that Susan was diagnosed with cervical cancer. The deed, still in the hands of her husband, became an albatross for her. She had no source of income: Hickory Hill was the only security she had in order to protect her children and herself. And so, in order to secure her rights Susan filed for divorce in Fairfax County on May 3, 1922.[11]

In her "bill of complaint," Susan asked that the Hickory Hill deed, which remained in the hands of her husband, not be recorded. She also requested that its transfer to her husband be cancelled, and that title to the 77 acre property be restored to her. She strongly felt that her husband might record the deed and attempt to dispose or remove some of the property or to encumber it. She asked for an immediate restraining order regarding the deed and for herself, insisting that her husband was dangerous and might do her serious harm once the divorce papers were recorded. The same day she filed for divorce, the court issued an injunction against her husband so that he could not record the deed, encumber the tract of land, dispose or remove furniture, household items, other personal property or step foot on the Hickory Hill estate.[12]

However, Speer had a way of obtaining what he wanted. On May 6, 1922, just three days after filing for divorce, Susan rewrote her will which was witnessed by Douglass Sorrell Mackall, Jr., and his brother John. Both men were lawyers who also resided in the Langley area of McLean. In this new will Susan left everything to her husband and assigned him the role of sole executer:

"WILL OF SUSAN V. SPEER

I, Susan V. Speer, of Fairfax County, Virginia, do hereby make, publish and declare this to be my last will and testament, hereby revoking any and all former wills and codicils by me at any time heretofore made.

First – I give, devise and bequeath unto my husband, Dr. James P. Speer, all of the property and estate, real, personal and mixed, now owned or hereafter acquired by me, and of which I shall die seized and possessed, absolutely and in fee simple to him and his heirs forever.

Second - I do hereby nominate, constitute and appoint my husband, Dr. James P. Speer of Fairfax County, Virginia, sole executer of this my last will and testament, and request that he be authorized to qualify and act as such without giving hand.

WITNESS my hand and seal this 6th day of May, A. D. 1922.

Susan V. Speer     (Seal)

Signed, sealed, published and declared by Susan V. Speer as and for her last will and testament in the presence of us, who, in her presence, and at her request, and in the presence each other, having signed names as subscribing witnesses to said will.

D. S. Mackall, Jr.
John C. Mackall[13]"

Seven months after turning everything over to her husband, Susan died at Hickory Hill on January 12, 1923.[15] She was cremated and her funeral service took place at Hickory Hill. On two occasions, before her death, Susan rewrote her will: the first change took place on October 30, 1922, and the second alteration was a codicil to her last will and statement dated December 18, 1922.[16] Her husband contested the will maintaining she didn't have had the mental capacity to prepare a will/codicil due to the medication (morphine) she was taking to help relieve the pain. The wills underwent probate and a jury of seven persons decided the outcome on May 28, 1923: the jury consisted of Carlin Cockrell; Alvin Rich; Silas Hutchison; E. E. Gillette; Samuel Styles; W. W. Watkins; and W. R. Watkins, all of whom resided in Fairfax County. After reviewing the wills behind closed doors, the jury returned to the courtroom and submitted the following decision:

> "We the Jury upon this issues joined find that the will dated May 6, 1922 is the true last will and testament of Susan V. Speer and that the will dated Oct. 20, 1922, is not the true last will and testament of Susan V. Speer and that the codicil dated Dec. 18, 1922, is not a valid codicil of the last will and testament of Susan V. Speer.
>
> E. E. Gillette    Foreman[17]"

Speer was now in absolute ownership of Hickory Hill. A little over a year after Susan's death he wed Dora Armstrong Starr, a divorcee with one child named Armstrong Starr. The wedding took place on March 16, 1924, in Alexandria at the Methodist Church. The *Evening Star* printed the following:

> "Dr. James P. Speer of McLean and Dora E. Starr of Washington were married at Alexandria, Va March 16, by Rev. Robert E. Browne of the Methodist Church. Dr. Speer's son, Ira L. Speer of Washington, and his brother, Dr. T. Spencer Speer, were the only attendants at the wedding. Dr. and Mrs. Speer will make their home at Hickory Hill. McLean."[18]

An existing debt of $10,000 still remained on the estate. On April 14, 1924, Eppe McFarland, of Loudoun County, loaned the Speers $10,000 for three years, in order to eliminate the debt. This included interest and Hickory Hill was used as collateral. The property was held in trust by Edwin Garrett and Walter Oliver McFarland. The Speers found the obligation too burdensome. Frank Lyon, whose estate "Franklyon Farm" joined the Speer's land, came to their rescue and purchased the 77 acre Hickory Hill property on October 16, 1924. As part of the purchase price, Lyon assumed and agreed to pay off the existing $10,000 loan through a deed of trust with Douglass and John Mackall.[19] It is interesting to note that Susan, Speer's first wife, was the legal sole purchaser of Hickory Hill, but both Speer and his second wife Dora jointly owned the property and were the sellers.[20] Speer's outlandish lifestyle eventually caught up with him. He died of a fatal heart attack in Washington D. C. on March 20, 1925,[21] at the Roosevelt Hotel, just five months after Hickory Hill was sold to Lyon.

In 1998, at age 85, Virginia Speer Grovermann, the youngest daughter of Susan and Pat Speer, wrote to Ethel Kennedy, Hickory Hill's owner at that time, describing the house and grounds of the estate as she remembered them. She stated that the house had a slate mansard roof, a cupola and a screened porch. There was no running water or electricity when her family moved into the house, but it was installed shortly thereafter. Grovermann went on to add that her brothers hauled stone from the back of the property for building the stone wall in front of the house along Chain Bridge Road. She also included two photographs: one is of the house during the period she lived there and one depicts the house sitting vacant before the Lyons redesigned and renovated it. Grovermann's letter, in part, follows:

Dear Mrs. Kennedy:

I am enclosing some pictures I have of Hickory Hill when I lived there from 1914 to 1925.* There were originally two porches of ornate gingerbread on the front and side entrances. My father had the screened in porch put on and we enjoyed many happy days and evenings there. This is what we did in those days – sitting and sometimes listening to the phonograph as there were no radio or tv then.

The first floor had a living room, the library (or den), a dining room, a huge kitchen and pantry. The second floor had five bedrooms and one bathroom. The third floor had four bedrooms, one bath and a stairway leading up to a cupola on top of the house.

The first picture with sports car shows how it looked when we lived there. The second picture shows how it looked after my father sold it. It was standing empty and sad. My sister (far left) and her friends had taken a drive out to 'home' as we called it.

The building on the right of the house is the 'well house' where the Deleo system pumped water. When we moved there, there was no running water or electricity. This was all installed. The wall around the front was contracted to Ace B. Steuart of D.C., who was a brick layer. My two brothers hauled the stones from the back of the barn where a silo had been years ago. My brothers always said 'no one could tear that wall down, not even the Kennedys.' Notice the cement forms on the pillars of the wall – they did not last long as my parents preferred the simpler wall. There was 150 acres to this property where now stands many homes. Remember this was the days of farm property and around us were many big farms such as ours.*

Not too far from the house was a 'cool house' as we called it. It was where we kept the fresh milk, butter, cream, and buttermilk as we had many cows. Also, work horses, riding horses, pigs, chickens, geese, and my pony. It was always cool there and cemented with troughs for huge dairy utensils. As I remember there were two rooms, one for the milk, etc. and the other for barrels of pickles, sower kraut, etc. I used to love to go down there and dip my fingers into that heavy cream. I love it to this day. There was a chicken house, smoke house, and huge barn and a special barn for the riding horses. There was a huge garden, wheat fields, corn fields, and oat fields. The garden is where you have your pool and bath houses. There were two tennis courts beautifully maintained and of course we played tennis. There was an orchard of apples, pears, plums, peaches, and quince….

McLean was just a little village then with a Justice of Peace and Mr. Storm's general store – mostly groceries. My sister who had her riding horse and I on my pony used to ride all over McLean, especially, to Black Pond which was supposed to have no bottom, where we all learned to swim – also down Chain Bridge Road to Chain Bridge where the young dare devils (the young men) used to jump off the <u>old</u> bridge into the Potomac. The Potomac was beautiful in those days and many people had their cottages on its sandy beaches. Hard to believe, isn't it.

My father, Dr. James Patrick Speer, was a dentist and he practiced dentistry in D.C. He and my mother had six children, three boys and three girls. We were a very happy family; however, tragedy struck us when my mother who was only 40 passed on there at Hickory Hill. After my mother's passing he did not want to live at Hickory Hill so he sold it to Mr. Lyon of Lyon Village in Clarendon, Va. Mr. Lyon sold it to a man (can't think of his name) who had an automobile agency in D.C. and he in turn sold it to Justice Jackson and you know the rest of the story. I don't know if this is really accurate or not but it's the way I remember it.

The Speer family have all passed on now – I am the last one. – I'm the Baby – and I'm 85 years old. I did want to mention the car in the driveway in the picture. I think it was a Ford Templar?? Anyway it was my father's gift to his middle son for passing all of his subjects at school. My brothers all attended Randolph Macon Academy (a school in Southern Virginia. Most all of the young middle class boys in the area and D.C. attended Randolph Macon. Washington, D.C. was a little country town then, shady and beautiful, sleepy and serene. All the old families knew each other and we would drive in on Saturday evening, park the car on "F" Street and promenade and see all of our friends. We would have dinner at the Willard, attend Keith's vaudeville show, pancakes at Childs and go home. What a life – I'll always cherish the memories – such happy ones.

I hope you enjoy these pictures and I'm glad I had them to share with you. Always remember Hickory Hill is full of happy memories -----ENJOY! Life is beautiful.

My love,

Virginia Speer Grovermann"[22]

Grovermann's recollection of the dates she resided at Hickory Hill and the amount of acreage are not correct. The estate was purchased by Susan Speer in 1916 and sold by Patrick and Dora Armstrong Speer in 1924. At that time Hickory Hill consisted of 77 acres.

The cement design running atop the length of the stone wall was not removed by the Speers during their ownership of Hickory Hill. It remained after they sold the property as indicated in the lower photograph on the following page.

The above picture shows Hickory Hill during the time the Speer family resided there. Of interest, is the cement formation running along the top of the stone wall. It was replaced in later years and flattened with large slate slabs. The automobile appears to be a Templar touring car. The lower photo shows a Speer daughter (far left) with friends during an afternoon drive in the countryside. At this time Hickory Hill was under the ownership of Frank Lyon and the house was vacant.                                    (Virginia Speer Grovermann)

The Speer family poses with their six children for a photograph ca.1915. From left to right, the bottom row pictures James Patrick, Jr., Dr. James Patrick Speer, Ira, and Susan holding baby Virginia on her lap. The back row shows Madeline, Lucile and Spencer.

(Speer: Ancestry.com)

Storm's General Store and Post Office was the life line for McLean residents. It was located facing Chain Bridge Road adjacent to the tracks of the Great Falls and Old Dominion Railroad. (*McLean Remembers*)

# CHAPTER 7
## The Lyon/Fitch Years

Unlike George Walters, Frank Lyon was not born in Fairfax County, nor was his vocation that of a farmer: he was a lawyer, newspaper publisher and real estate developer. Lyon was born in Petersburg, Virginia, in 1867, and educated in Richmond. He attended the Georgetown School of Law at night, while also working as a stenographer with the Interstate Commerce Commission. In 1890 he married Georgia (Georgie) Hays Wright whose father, John Vines Wright, was a land office attorney and had been a member of Congress prior to the Civil War. In 1892 Lyon began to practice law in Alexandria County and, later, became a law partner with Robert Walton Moore, who, at this time, was a land speculator and developer. Moore introduced Lyon to the real estate business. At that time Alexandria County was largely rural, and land along the Potomac River was considered an unfit place to live. Lawless communities had developed along the Virginia shoreline between the Aqueduct and Long Bridges with names like Hell's Bottom, Dead Man's Hollow and St. Asaph's Race Track. They were strongholds of gambling casinos, pawnshops, saloons, drunkenness, brothels, murderers and other unsavory activities that served the vices of residents of both the District of Columbia and Virginia. As the situation worsened over the years, it became evident that Alexandria County needed to change its image by eliminating the illicit activities. Law and order needed to be established before development could begin in a meaningful manner.

At the beginning of the twentieth century Lyon became the editor/owner of Alexandria County's newspaper, *The Alexandria County Monitor*, through which he led a crusade to stamp out the "red light" district, and rid the county of its illicit activities.[1] In spite of his efforts, and those of others, little changed along the river. In desperation the commonwealth's attorney Crandal Mackey put together a small group of law abiding citizens in 1904 that included Lyon.[2] He deputized everyone, obtained warrants and headed up a posse armed with guns, axes and sledgehammers in an attempt to destroy the numerous illegal businesses. The raiders wrecked every gambling establishment along the Potomac between Alexandria and the Aqueduct Bridge.[3] The lawlessness did not end at that time, but the raid provided a strong beginning, and eventually Mackey succeeded in shutting down the unlawful establishments. This helped to change the character of the environment along the river from an unsavory-filled atmosphere to that of industry, business and a place where people wanted to live. On May 1, 1905, *The Washington Star* printed:

> "Thanks to the vigor of a new county administration, the gamblers have been forced to leave the southern side of the river....No longer need there be degrading conditions on the high road from the city to the national cemetery or at the very gates of the military post, both of which are of instructive interest to all visitors to this city. It will be possible for tourists to inspect both of these points without being subjected to disgusting sights or unpleasant experiences."

Besides joining the movement to eliminate vice along the river, Lyon used his newspaper to vigorously campaign against liquor, and when petitions were filed on April 29, 1905, for liquor licenses in Alexandria County Lyon was hired to represent the dry forces in court. He successfully argued against granting such licenses by using a little-known legislative clause in the liquor licensing law that suggested liquor licenses should not be granted without adequate police protection. At that time the police security in Alexandria County consisted of one sheriff and one deputy. The dry forces won: Judge C. E. Nichol did not grant the licenses.[4] Thus, the saloons were closed down and sale of liquor by the drink ended in Alexandria County. The land speculators and reformers had basically cleared the county from its illegal and criminal activities, paving the way for real estate development in the area.

Before the vice was eliminated along the river, development had already started in Alexandria County for a new community called Clarendon. Lyon's law partner Moore acquired a large parcel of land adjacent to this development and, in 1910 the two men began platting a 300 acre extension of the area known as "Moore's Addition at Clarendon." Moore was later elected to Congress by a special election held on April 22, 1919, and sold his interest in the property to Lyon, who then proceeded to create Lyon Park. The following year, Lyon partnered with Charles Walton Fitch to form the development firm Lyon & Fitch. The company was later renamed Lyon Properties, Inc. Fitch, who was about 13 years younger than Lyon, was married to Margaret Lyon Parham, a niece of Lyon. He was a graduate of Cornell University, and had served in Europe during World War I, returning with the rank of lieutenant colonel. Together they began to promote and develop Lyon Park into a new large residential subdivision for families of modest means in what was no longer known as Alexandria County. Virginia's General Assembly voted in 1920 to change this portion of the county to Arlington County to avoid the continuing confusion with the adjacent City of Alexandria. The new county's accessibility to Washington City made it a very desirable place for a person to own a home. Advertisements were placed in various newspapers beginning in 1920. Below are two such announcements for Lyon Park: the first was printed in the *Evening Star* on May 3, 1920, and the lower advertisement appeared in the *Richmond Times Dispatch* on August 1, 1920.

"LYON PARK (VINSON STATION), THE beautiful new addition to Clarendon, Va,: 20 minutes' ride from the Post Office Department, 12th and Pa, ave., on the Falls Church line. HOUSES, LOTS and ACREAGE for sale on easy terms. Lots, $7.50 cash, $7.50 month. Lyon Park has cement sidewalks, sewers, gas, electricity and native trees. See Mr. Fitch about building a home. LYON & FITCH, Owners, on property." (*Evening Star* May 3, 1920)

"OVERLOOKING WASHINGTON, D.C. – For sale, fine building lots 3 miles from White House, on highlands on Virginia, at Lyon Park Arlington County: 20 minutes from heart of city over good roads or by excellent electric car service. All conveniences including cement sidewalks, sewers, gas and electricity: 50-foot lots for $15 case and $15 per month. Reference Citizens' National Bank of Alexandria, Va. Apply for further information to Lyon & Fitch. Owners. Clarendon, Va." (*Richmond Times Dispatch* August 1, 1920)

Previous to acquiring the vast piece of property that developed into Lyon Park, Lyon purchased at public auction 12.538 acres adjacent to Clarendon in 1904 for a price of $500 per acre. This was subdivided and became known as "Lyon's Addition to Clarendon."[5] Any purchaser of a lot in Lyon Park and "Lyon's Addition to Clarendon" had to agree not to sell or dispense alcohol or liquor in any form on the property.[6]

While the area was still called Alexandria County, Lyon purchased several parcels in the area of today's 25th Street and Old Dominion Drive and combined them. In 1907 he took 20 acres of this acquisition and built a large residence where he lived with his wife Georgie and their three children: Georgie, John and Margaret. The house was architecturally built in a Spanish-style, with a rough sand finish, red tiled roof and surrounded by wide porches. An additional feature built near the house was a large tower used to store water. Not at all modest, Lyon named his residence Lyonhurst.[7] A subdivision built around the house was named Lyonhurst and the road (today's 25th Street) leading to the house was accordingly named Lyonhurst Avenue. Lyonhurst was one of the first homes in Alexandria County to have electric power. The house was built near the tracks of the electrified Great Falls and Old Dominion Railroad which ran from Rosslyn to Great Falls Park. Lyon was able to purchase excess power from the rail line. Ruth Rose, an Arlington County historian, described the Lyons use of electricity:

> "...The trolley line had an excess of power and the company decided to sell some of the power to landowners along the line. The Lyons' were among the first to take advantage of the electricity. During the morning and evening rush hours, however, the amount of power was diminished because of the frequency of the trains. The Lyons' electric stove was of little use to them during the breakfast and dinner hours because those hours coincided with the train's rush hours."[8]

Three significant events involved the Lyon family during their residency at Lyonhurst. On October 18, 1911, Lyonhurst was the site of the wedding of their oldest daughter, Georgie, to Lieutenant Jacob L. Devers,[9] a West Point graduate who years later retired as a four star general. A second wedding took place on May 22, 1917, in the garden at Lyonhurst with the marriage of their second daughter, Margaret, to Charles Walton Smith.[10] Smith graduated from law school at George Washington University in 1913 and was employed at the Land Office of the Department of Interior. After marrying Margaret he became a law partner with her father and later took on the duties of secretary-treasurer of the real estate development firm Lyon & Fitch. The Lyon's son John never married. In 1918, as a 25 year old lieutenant during World War I, he lost his life in Argonne, France. A special "Home Coming Edition" of *The Monitor* was printed on September 1, 1919, honoring the soldiers of Alexandria County who were returning from the War. The following story was featured on the front page, but according to Rose, it contained two errors: Lyon was a first lieutenant when he died and he had attended law school at George Washington University:

> "John Lyon was killed in action on October 16, 1918. He was second lieutenant in the 29th Division in the Machine Gun Company of the 116th Infantry. He was a graduate of Western High School, attended the University of Virginia for two years, editor of the Alexandria County Monitor for two years, at the same time attending Georgetown Law School at night, but did not graduate owing to the fact that he went to France in May, just before had had completed his examinations. He served one year with the American Ambulance Corps in France, and was assistant editor of Forest and Stream in New York. He served six months on the Mexican border. He entered the Army through the Alexandria Light Infantry, in which he volunteered as a common soldier, was promoted from corporal to sergeant and to second lieutenant, and reached France July 1918."[11]

The development of Lyon Park was largely successful due to the influx of government employees that remained in the area after World War I and advances in local transportation such as street car lines. Trolleys, such as the Great Falls and Old Dominion Railroad, provided a reliable and inexpensive mode of transportation for commuters living in the growing suburbs. And so, Lyon, as a pioneering developer, began looking for additional real estate to purchase. He found 165 acres formerly used for a dairy farm which he bought from the descendants of Robert Cruit in 1923 for $185,000.[12] The property was then platted by Lyon & Fitch which sold the lots at a price between $1600 and $2400 for the development of Lyon Village.[13] This was a planned residential community of single family dwellings where the purchaser of a lot built his own home. Cruit purchased the property in 1825 to operate a farm. His farmhouse was not destroyed and remains today on Highland Street. Lyon's interest in acquiring additional real estate in Arlington basically ended with the platting and development of Lyon Village. His attention then turned to that of becoming a gentleman farmer in nearby Fairfax County.

In 1919, the same year that Lyon acquired Moore's interest in "Moore's Addition at Clarendon," the Lyons bought 63 acres in the Langley area of McLean which included the pre-Civil War farmhouse of William Muse that had descended to the Abner Stephenson family. The Lyons acquisition abutted both the Hickory Hill and Salona properties.[43] The roots of their purchase originated in 1911 when a widow, Katharine Fleming, acquired the estate. As part of her purchase price, she assumed a $3000 deed of trust, plus interest, signed in 1905 between Alfred and William Spahr with George Gunnell. One of the trustees was Lyon's law partner Moore.[15] Fleming defaulted on the payment of the entire amount of the loan and the title was conveyed to Moore in February of 1915.[16] In order for Gunnell to receive his money, it was necessary for the property to be auctioned off at the Fairfax County Courthouse. The auction took place on January 18, 1919, and Douglass Sorrell Mackall was the highest bidder at $3650.[17] A little over three months later, on April 24, 1919, Lyon purchased the 63 acre tract from Mackall for $8500.[18]

The Lyons continued to live at Lyonhurst, but after the marriage of their two daughters and the death of their son in France, they found themselves to be "empty nesters." Possibly this is a reason they elected to leave Lyonhurst for the nearby countryside in Fairfax County. The Great Falls and Old Dominion Railroad that ran in front of Lyonhurst continued through McLean with numerous stops along the line, giving the Lyons access to Arlington and Georgetown. In 1922 Lyonhurst was sold to Dr. Richard Sutton,[19] but it was not until the following year that the Lyons left Lyonhurst and moved out to nearby rural McLean. They settled into the existing farmhouse on their property while awaiting the completion of a magnificent home they were having built. Lyon purchased an additional adjoining 13.8 acres along Pimmit Run, a Potomac tributary, from Ward Kirby on October 20, 1922,[20] and much of the house was constructed with stone quarried from the stream.[21] The Lyons moved into their new house after it was completed in 1924. In keeping with the Lyon style, the estate was named the Franklyon Farm.[22]

The house was an elegant Georgian stone mansion based upon designs by Charles Ashmead Fuller.[23] It contained 16 main rooms, four baths and an unfinished third floor.[24] Fuller was not an architect by profession: he worked in the fields of real estate and banking. He spent a good deal of his time on the golf course, becoming one of the area's leading golfers and several times champion at the Chevy Chase Club. However, his father, Thomas J. D. Fuller, was an early notable architect in the District of Columbia. Possibly Fuller drew up the plans with the help of his father and Lyon approved them.

The 1920s was a decade of economic prosperity. Lifestyles changed as people across the nation began leaving their farms for life in the city. Owning a car, radio and your own home were aspirations for many families. Lyon & Fitch prospered as their lots were sold and affordable homes were built. Lyon enjoyed life as a "gentleman farmer," but continued with his law practice in Washington while Fitch and Smith oversaw the real estate operations, along with Lawrence Mitchael who helped with sales.[25]

Lyon was serious about raising a quality dairy herd which consisted of registered Guernsey cattle. Perhaps his interest in farming led him to increase his personal real estate holdings by buying the adjoining Hickory Hill property from the Speers on October 16, 1924.[26] Soon thereafter, the acreage of Hickory Hill and the Franklyon Farm were significantly altered: Lyon took approximately 71 acres from the Hickory Hill property and added them to Franklyon Farm. The size of the Hickory Hill estate was now reduced to 5.6975 acres and the size of Franklyon Farm was increased to 145.22 acres. Furthermore, Franklyon Farm now surrounded Hickory Hill in a U shaped pattern.[27]

After Lyon's purchase, Hickory Hill remained vacant for roughly a year-and-a half, before it was sold to his partner Fitch on March 19, 1926, for $20,000.[28] Just a few weeks later, on April 2, 1926, Lyon completed the last of his payments on the $10,000 deed of trust taken out for the purchase of Hickory Hill,[29] and Fitch, along with his wife Margaret, moved into the house with their four children: Mary, Margaret, Martha, and Walton.

The Franklyon Farm quickly gained a highly respectable reputation throughout Fairfax County for its agricultural activities. For instance, at the 1927 Fairfax County Fair, Franklyon Farm was judged second in almost every category of the Cattle Division. It lost only to Kenilworth Farm, also of McLean, which had consistently won that division since 1920. The *Fairfax Herald* reported:

## "CATTLE

In pure bred Guernseys, Kenilworth Farm of McLean carried off top honors. Best bulls, 3 years and over, first and $5 special went to Kenilworth Farm. Best bull 1 year and under 2 went to Franklyon Farm, Langley: second Kenilworth Farm: third C. H. Speer, Oakton: fourth, Henry Magarity, McLean....

Best cows 3 years and over – First, Kenilworth Farm: second, Franklyon Farm: third and fourth, E. M. Palmer, Arlington....

Best heifer 18 months to 2 years – First, Kenilworth Farm: second, Franklyon Farm: third, Kenilworth Farm: fourth, Franklyon Farm.

Best heifer (junior yearling) – First, Kenilworth Farm: second and third, Franklyon Farm: fourth, Kenilworth Farm....

Best heifer (junior calf) – First, Franklyon Farm: second, third, and fourth, Kenilworth Farm."[30]

In October of 1929 the stock market collapsed, setting off a never before seen wave of financial panic across America. By the middle of the following year, the Great Depression was in full swing. There was a national collapse in real estate values, land development and residential construction, forcing the break-up of Lyon & Fitch. The Lyons sold the Franklyon Farm for $65,000 on November 12, 1930, to Fred Van Vranken and Edward Wissman, two young real estate salesmen who lived in the District of Columbia,[31] and moved into Georgetown. Van Vranken and Wissman were unable to maintain the loan payments. The Lyons regained the Franklyon Farm and, shortly thereafter, sold it to Percy Crosby, author and cartoonist, in 1932 for $85,000.[32]

The Fitches conveyed the 5.6975 acre Hickory Hill estate back to the Lyons on November 24, 1930,[33] and relocated to Chicago where Fitch became the Director of Exhibits for the 1933 Chicago World Fair. Sometime during the following year the Lyons proceeded to change Hickory Hill. The inside was gutted[34] and its outside appearance was transformed from a mansard roof style structure, with an encircling columned verandah, into a simpler two-and-a-half story white brick residence.[35] It has been suggested that Fuller once again assisted with the design.[36]

Lyon acquired additional property in Fairfax County on March 3, 1936, by purchasing 20 acres in a different section of McLean along the Lewinsville-Falls Church Road (today's Great Falls Street) and began building a home they named Green Pastures.[37] Hickory Hill was placed on the real estate market and on October 12, 1936, it was sold to a young couple, Leo and Leonora Rocca.[38] The Lyons relocated to Georgetown while their new home was being built; when it was finished, the Lyons left Georgetown and moved back to McLean. The life of a gentleman farmer was now a thing of the past for Lyon. The land surrounding Green Pastures was used primarily to pasture riding horses.[39]

The above photo shows Hickory Hill ca.1925. It was taken by Charles Fitch before Frank Lyon changed it into a simpler white brick residence without an encircling porch. The bottom picture is a ca.1942 photo of the Georgian style stone house Lyon completed in 1924 and named the Franklyon Farm. In later years the name was changed to Ballantrae.
(Top: Fairfax County Department of Planning and Zoning)        (Bottom: *McLean Remembers Again)*

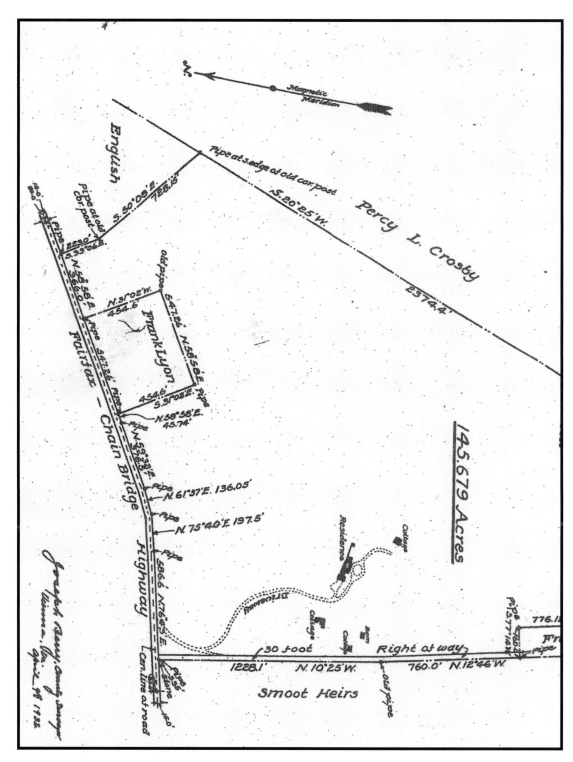

Hickory Hill was under the ownership of Frank Lyon when this plat was drawn by Joseph Berry in 1932. It shows a much reduced Hickory Hill in acreage after Lyon took 71 acres in 1924 and added them to his adjoining Franklyon Farm. Note how Hickory Hill is surrounded by the Lyon farm. The area labeled residence is the house Lyon built known today as Ballantrae.

(Fairfax County Public Library Archival Division)

After purchasing property that became a part of Arlington County, Frank Lyon, a lawyer and real estate developer, platted Lyon Village and Lyon Park. He moved to McLean in 1923 and, using stones from Pimmit Run, built a magnificent home, upon what was named the Franklyon Farm. He purchased the adjoining Hickory Hill estate in 1924 and reduced its size by 71 acres by adding them to the Franklyon Farm. Later, he renovated Hickory Hill and, in the process, changed the outside appearance of the red brick house by changing the roof line and painting the bricks white. (Arlington County Public Library)

Georgie Hays Wright, whose father John Vines Wright served as a member of the House of Representatives for the 7th Congressional District of Tennessee prior to the Civil War, married Frank Lyon in 1890.

(Arlington County Public Library)

First Lieutenant John Lyon was killed during action at Argonne, France, while attempting to rescue a wounded officer. A monument honoring him and three other soldiers killed in World War I was dedicated in Cherrydale, Arlington County on April 25, 1926. Veterans of Foreign Wars, John Lyon Post 3150, maintains the memorial and every year conducts ceremonies at the monument on Memorial Day and Veterans Day.

(Top: John Lyon Post 3150)   (Bottom: Carole Herrick)

In 1907, Frank Lyon began building a Spanish style stucco residence for his family in Alexandria County. He named it Lyonhurst. A large tower to store water (shown below) was included and can be seen in the background through the trees in the above picture. Today it is known as Missionhurst and currently serves as the headquarters for the Immaculate Heart Mission Fathers.                                    (Both: Carole Herrick)

General Jacob L. Devers, husband of Georgie Hays Lyon, was commander of the United States forces in the European Theater of Operations during World War II; he retired a four star general. He is shown in 1943 as a Lt. General decorating Lt. Colonel Frank Capra with the Legion of Merit Award for his production of motion pictures that led to the United States entry into World War II.

(Library of Congress)

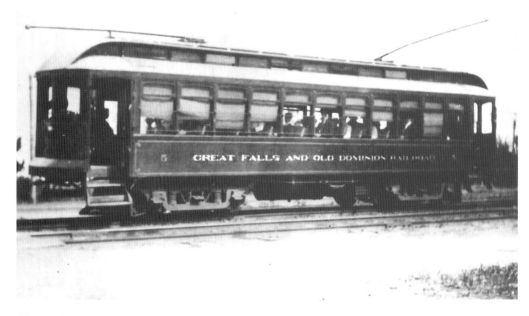

Shown is a passenger car of the Great Falls and Old Dominion Railroad, a trolley line that operated between Rosslyn and the Great Falls. The Lyons purchased excess electricity from the rail line while living at Lyonhurst. (*Rails to the Blue Ridge*)

# CHAPTER 8
## The Rocca Residency

Leo Rocca was a native Washingtonian. As a young man he attended St. Patrick's Church, served in the Student Army Training Corps during World War I, graduated from the Business High School and went to George Washington University.[1] His professional career spanned 25 years in the rapidly growing automotive industry. Rocca began his automotive career by selling various parts for automobiles. In August of 1919, at age 21, he formed an association with his brother-in-law Michael O'Hanlon and they opened a repair shop on N Street, N.E. in the District. This was the perfect time for entrepreneurial involvement in such a venture as the nation was rapidly changing from the days of the horse and buggy to that of the horseless carriage. In 1921 the pair organized a Ford dealership called the Triangle Motor Company which was located at New York Avenue and North Capitol Street.[2] At that time there were eight other authorized Ford dealers in Washington. Besides the Triangle Motor Company, they included R. L. Taylor Company, Universal Auto Company, Donohoe Motor Company, Hill & Tibbits, Parkway Motor Company, Robey Motor Company, Strobel Motor Company and Steuart's Garage.[3] The following is an advertisement that ran in the *Evening Star* newspaper July 16, 1922:

**"FORDS – FORDS.**
**Touring – Choice of several**

Coupes – Choice of 3 ........................... $135 up
Sedans – Choice of several................... $425
Runabout – New body A1 .................... $275
Runabout – Runs O.K............................ $90
Speedster – Very classy........................ $190

Easy terms
Triangle Motor Company
No. 3 – 5 – 7 New York Ave., N. E."

From the beginning, the Triangle Motor Company witnessed a rapid increase in business and, so, the stockholders decided to enlarge in 1922 by constructing a three-story building on the New York Avenue location at a cost of $35,000. In 1924 the company further expanded at the same site by erecting another building on the property at a cost of approximately $100,000[4] and continued its Ford operations there. For a brief time in 1927, Rocca ventured into the business of barnstorming and flying passengers in Ford tri-motor airplanes.[5]

> " All known records for passenger sightseeing flights from an American airport were broken here yesterday by Washington airport and by Hoover Field.... A large portion of the Washington Airport passenger flying was done by a visiting Ford tri-motored transport plane owned by Leo Rocca of this city. All of the flights were regular sightseeing trips over the city and the bulk of the passengers were tourists paying Easter visits to the National Capital."[6]

In January of 1934 Rocca dissolved his ties with the Triangle Motor Company to become an independent automobile dealer.[7] That same year he formed Leo Rocca, Inc., a direct factory dealership for Dodge and Plymouth cars and trucks at New York Avenue and North Capitol Street.[8] As Dodge and Plymouth vehicles were sweeping the nation in popularity, his sales were strong, and Leo Rocca, Inc. kept pace with the growing demand to quickly become a leader in the fiercely competitive field. Also, in 1934, Leo Rocca, Inc. saw advantages in selling used vehicles and leased ground at the corner of Fourth Street and Florida Avenue for the Union Market Terminal, a used car lot.[9]

Leo Rocca, Inc. relocated to 4301 Connecticut Avenue N. W., where there was a large showroom, auto repair garage and gasoline filling station. As World War II approached, there was an acute shortage of male workers in the Washington area due to the draft. Rocca was having difficulty getting help at his automobile agency, but in particular with the filling station. Nothing came of advertisements and, so, he came up with the innovative idea of hiring young women to pump gasoline for customers. These women also cleaned windows and checked automotive essentials such as oil and tire air pressure. They wore a uniform which consisted of white rubber-soled shoes, red socks, a pleated wool blue crepe skirt, a white middy blouse and a red tie.[10] Women had never done this type of work before. They were quite successful and brought in a good deal of business.

Rocca married Leonora Lucille Worley of Chevy Chase, Maryland, in the spring of 1930.[11] The couple resided in the Rock Creek Hills section of Washington and after starting a family, Leo Jr. and Leonora Starr, they decided to move out to the Virginia countryside. On October 24, 1936, the Rocca's purchased the 5.6975 acre Hickory Hill property from the Lyons.[12] The house was the residence that Lyon had remodeled in 1931 converting Walters' mansard roof red brick dwelling into a simpler two-and-a-half story white brick residence. Hickory trees continued to line the driveway and a vast amount of green lawn surrounded the house. The following article appeared in the *Evening Star* on September 19, 1936, relating that the 175 year old Hickory Hill had been purchased by the Rocca's. The inaccuracy of the date suggests that the house was built ca.1761. It appears that the author just threw out a date that sounded good and did not do research:

> " Leo Rocca, Capital automobile dealer, has purchased an estate near Langley, Va., Fairfax County, it was announced today. The property includes six acres of landscaped grounds and garden and a 175 year-old colonial brick residence.
>
> The estate adjoins the property of Percy Crosby, cartoonist, on the Langley-Fairfax road. Rocca intends to sell his present home, located at 1735 Holly Street, in Rock Creek Hills."

The Rocca's made some minor changes to the house and also converted an old Chevrolet automobile into a tractor which was used for mowing the lawn. They did not keep cows, but did have a large vegetable garden and some fruit trees. Lenora liked to can and preserved much of what was grown through canning.[13] Leo loved the house and wanted to be in the country; however, they lived at Hickory Hill less than five years. Their activities, whether it was social, church, business or their children's education, took place in the District and the shortest route into the District and to Leo Rocca, Inc. involved crossing the Chain Bridge. The Potomac's record breaking flood of 28.10 feet at Little Falls,[14] which still holds today, took place on March 19, 1936, before the Rocca's purchased Hickory Hill.[15] Chain Bridge, which had been dangerous to cross for several years, did not fall. Astonishingly there was minimal damage to the structure. It was determined that the foundations were sound and after a few necessary repairs, the bridge would be safe to cross. The bridge underwent the required patchwork and reopened on May 29, 1936.[16] However, the Potomac's third highest flood occurred on April 28, 1937, cresting at 23.7 feet.[17] The bridge held, but, having been built in 1874, it was clear that it was time to replace it. Dismantling of the Chain Bridge began on August 19, 1937, and the dedication of the new bridge took place on June 17, 1938.[18] Perhaps the fact that most of the Rocca's activities were in the District, combined with the unreliability of the Chain Bridge, influenced their decision to move back to Washington. Whatever the reason, Hickory Hill was sold to Robert and Irene Jackson on July 9, 1941.[19] The sale price was $47,950.[20] A descriptive advertisement for the sale of Hickory Hill by the Rocca's printed in the *Evening Star* on March 23, 1941:

## "HICKORY HILL

> Lovely old Colonial brick mansion in historic Virginia's fine estate section, yet only 20 minutes from downtown Washington over the most unspoiled drive into the city. Six-acre expanse of fine lawn and gardens and hundreds of boxwood and other valuable shrubs. Giant old hickory, oak, walnut and spruce trees around the house and grounds. This beautiful home has retained all the charm of Colonial days although completely modernized as to plumbing, heating, etc. Especially economical to heat and keep up. Nicely equipped stable for riding horses. Price, $52,500. Can finance with $17,000 cash payment for substantial purchaser. Inspection by appointment only. Apply your own broker or LEO J. ROCCA, Chestnut 4725."

A few months later a notice appeared in the *Evening Star* on July 17, 1941, announcing the purchase of Hickory Hill by Justice Robert H. Jackson. It is interesting to compare this article with the *Evening Star's* September 19, 1936, purchase of Hickory Hill by the Rocca's. The 1936 version suggested that the house was over 175 years old; thus, providing its construction a date of ca.1761. The later account printed below claims that the house was 100 years old, giving it a date ca.1841. Not only are both dates incorrect, but there is an 80 year difference between the two stories, which were written roughly five years apart. Having been constructed ca.1870 by George Walters, Hickory Hill was 71 years old when the Jackson's made their purchase. The small 1941 article erroneously reported the following:

## "Justice Jackson Gets
## Deed to Historic Estate

Special Dispatch to The Star.
FAIRFAX, Va., July 17, - A deed conveying Hickory Hill, historic estate in the Langley area of Fairfax County, Va., to Justice Robert H. Jackson was filed today with County clerk John M. Whalen at the county courthouse here.

The estate, which is believed to be 100 years old, was sold to Justice Jackson by Leo J. Rocca, Washington automobile dealer. The sale price was $47,950."

Leo Rocca, bottom left, is shown with other Washington D. C. Ford and Lincoln dealers in 1924.
(*Washington Post*)

This is a photo of Hickory Hill about the time it was sold by the Rocca's to the Jacksons.
(John Q. Barrett)

# CHAPTER 9
## The Jackson Residency

Robert H. Jackson was a successful lawyer who was born in 1892 on the family farm in Spring Creek Township, Pennsylvania. Not long after his birth, the Jackson family moved to Frewsburg, a quiet community just over the state line in western New York. After graduating from Frewsburg High School in 1909, Jackson furthered his education another year by attending nearby Jamestown High School, where he received a second high school diploma in 1910. After graduating he did not attend college, but instead studied as an apprentice lawyer in Jamestown. After a year of apprenticeship, he enrolled at the Albany Law School in order to get his law degree. He completed the law course in one year, but the school would not grant him a diploma because he was not yet 21 years of age. Reaching the required age in 1913, Jackson took and passed the New York bar examination; he then joined a law firm in Jamestown.

Jackson practiced law in the state of New York for 16 years before moving to Washington, D. C. in 1934 with his wife, Irene, and their two children, William and Mary. He began his Washington career by serving as General Counsel of the Bureau of Revenue in the United States Department of Treasury. He briefly remained in that position before moving to the Securities and Exchange Commission. In 1936 he served as the Assistant Attorney General in charge of the Tax Division of the Department of Justice and in 1937 became the Assistant Attorney General of its Anti-Trust Division. Jackson was a man on the move. In 1938 he became Solicitor General of the United States, serving as the government's chief spokesman before the United States Supreme Court. Then, in January of 1940, Jackson took the oath of office for Attorney General of the United States, thus, assuming governance of the Department of Justice. Jackson was a very popular personality and a highly regarded player in the inner circles of President Franklin Roosevelt's New Deal programs, litigating against corporations and utilities holding companies. He participated in the 1934 prosecution of Samuel Insull, the 1935 income tax case against Andrew Mellon and the 1937 anti-trust case against Alcoa. There was even speculation in 1940 of a presidential ticket that would include Jackson as a vice-presidential running mate beside presidential candidate Secretary of State Cordell Hull if Roosevelt decided not to seek a third term.[1] Of course that did not happen; Roosevelt was elected to a third term and Jackson continued as Attorney General.

On June 2, 1941, the aging Chief Justice Charles Evans Hughes announced his retirement from the Supreme Court of the United States.[2] Roosevelt nominated Associate Justice Harlan Fiske Stone to replace Hughes as Chief Justice,[3] and selected Jackson to take the seat of Stone as an Associate Justice. The Jacksons realized they would probably be living in the greater Washington metropolitan area for some time if the nomination was confirmed. They had always rented during their years in Washington, but this latest appointment offered them an opportunity to look for a permanent residence. They moved quickly to find a home and, about a month later, purchased Hickory Hill. As seen in an advertisement that appeared in the *Washington Post* on October 13, 1940, the Rocca's had tried for several months to sell Hickory Hill prior to the Jacksons interest. This newspaper article did not claim that Hickory Hill was historic, but gave that impression by saying that the house was a beautifully restored residence; a sales price was not listed:

**"CHARMING INDEED**

'Hickory Hill,' in the estate section of scenic Fairfax County, where taxes are low, is the right answer if you desire proximity to Washington and the advantages of the country embodied in a home of refinement in an attractive setting with a wealth of splendid oaks and generous landscaping. The beautifully restored Colonial residence has 10 delightful rooms, 3 baths, and maid's quarters; and is a pleasant 20 minute drive by way of Chain Bridge to the State Department and vicinity.

For details and appointment to inspect,               FRANCES POWELL HILL
call Miss                                       1644 Connecticut Avenue
Fitch – COLumbia 4379 Sun.
and evenings, Decatur
3422 Week days."

By the time the Jacksons began their search for a home, the real estate firm in charge of Hickory Hill's sale had changed to Green & Magruder, realtors in Arlington County.[4] The Jacksons undoubtedly saw the advertisement placed in the *Washington Post* on June 15, 1941, briefly describing Hickory Hill, which stated the house was about 100 years old (ca.1841). When looking at the newspaper article on page 83 announcing that the Jacksons bought the 100 year-old Hickory Hill on July 9, 1941, one gets the impression that both articles were written by the same agent representing Green & Magruder. This individual did not do the necessary research. He/she relied on hearsay and embellished the history of the property. Hickory Hill is a post-Civil War house built by Walters. In 1841 Walters had not yet purchased the property or moved to Langley. The June 15 story read in part:

"'Hickory Hill,' one of the most interesting old houses in the Langley area of Fairfax County, is now being offered for sale through the office of Green & Magruder, Arlington County realtors. Built about 100 years ago with brick made on the place, it is generally believed that the house was constructed by the Walters family....

Another interesting tale is that two elderly women recently visited the place and, after asking permission to inspect the house which was their childhood home, sought an old bullet-ridden door. They explained to the present occupants that they amused themselves as children by prying bullets out of the dining room door. This door, however had been replaced when the house was restored several years ago....

'Hickory Hill' is built of solid brick, with 14-inch walls and partitions from the basement to the third floor. It contains seven fireplaces. The house originally had an underground tunnel from the basement to the cooling house.

The house is situated on a knoll in the center of a six-acre tract which is entirely in beautiful lawn adorned with huge old trees and numerous boxwood and shrubs. Fronting on Chain Bridge Road, the entire tract is surrounded by the large estate known as 'Ballantrae,' which at one time was owned by Percy Crosby, the cartoonist...."[5]

The Jacksons were a couple who enjoyed the rural atmosphere. Even though Hickory Hill was a good distance from the Supreme Court, they knew this was the house for them. They quickly moved forward to acquire the property, but were prudently cautious: they did not want to purchase a residence in the country and then have the nomination to the Supreme Court fall apart. This was a contingent purchase that was non-binding for both parties. On July 3, 1941, the Jacksons settled upon a purchase price of $47,950 and put down $5000, promising to pay the remainder at settlement or before August 1, 1941. On this same date, they executed a contingency memorandum of understanding with the Rocca's that itemized personal property that would be left behind and would then belong to the Jacksons once settlement was finalized. Included were such items as the lawn mower, trailer, tractor and large lawn urn, plus several items in the house that included the attic table and benches, gas stove and refrigerator in the kitchen, the piano in the hall, as well as the stair and master bedroom carpets. A careful Jackson even put in writing that "While I anticipate no such event, it is understood that I have no use for the property except in the event that my pending nomination is confirmed. In event of failure of confirmation, the purchase will not be effective."[6] In the long run, Jackson did not need to be concerned about confirmation. In less than a week, on July 7, 1941, the United States Senate approved Jackson as a justice of the Supreme Court.[7] Two days later, the Jacksons settled on obtaining Hickory Hill. The new justice issued a personal check in the amount of $43,018.97 for the remainder of the purchase price.[8] The Jacksons were now the new owners of Hickory Hill and it was not encumbered by debt.

Before moving into the two-and-a- half story house, the new owners immediately began the arduous task of remodeling it to suit their lifestyle. The Roccas had previously redesigned a living room by turning it into two rooms: the Jacksons decided to go back to the original format of a single room. The dining room was repapered in a blue Chippendale design and included a large fireplace, an antique mirror and an exquisite crystal chandelier that hung over the dining room table. The dining room opened into a kitchen that had all the modern conveniences of the time. There were five bedrooms, a recreation room paneled in knotty pine and guest quarters. The Jacksons loved the outdoors and horseback riding. A stable was built in back of the house that would accommodate at least three horses. Leading from the house were bridle paths along which the justice took daily horseback rides before going to the Supreme Court. There was a garden and he was frequently found there with spade, hoe and trowel. Jackson was proud of his garden and claimed that he had won the battle, fought by all gardeners, over weed and bug.[9] In a letter dated February 2, 1943, to Rocca, Jackson wrote, "While we were about it we took away the wood steps at the back of the house leading to the porch and to the dining room and had brick and stone treads put in."[10] The Jacksons moved from their Wardman Park apartment in the District into their newly renovated Hickory Hill by the first of October, 1941. This was just a few days shy of the start of his first term on the Supreme Court. The *Washington Post* described the renovated Hickory Hill:

"Mrs. Robert Jackson, wife of the Supreme Court Justice, will return to Washington with her daughter, Mary, shortly from their summer home in Jamestown, N.Y.

Upon their return, the Jacksons will be busy moving from their Wardman Park apartment into the historic home which they have bought near Langley, Va., Hickory Hill. The house which dates back to the Civil War days, is now undergoing remodeling. The two living rooms, which had been made into one by the former owner, are being put back in their original form.

The house, of early colonial architecture, is set in the midst of wooded grounds. Proof that the Jacksons are preparing to enjoy their country life is the badminton court – the English game is one of the former Attorney General's favorite pasttimes – and the newly built stables that are awaiting their three scheduled tenants.

A three-story establishment, the house combines the charm of the days of yore with the utility of modern design. An old-fashioned dining room, papered in a blue Chippendale design and featuring an exquisite crystal chandelier, large fireplace and an antique mirror, opens into a kitchen that is the ultimate in modernity.

The third floor is in the throes of remodeling but a recreation room paneled in knotty pine is already finished and guest quarters are well on their way to completion. The second floor is devoted exclusively to sleeping quarters, boasting five bedrooms.

Justice Jackson, who is already installed in his office in the Supreme Court Building, spends his leisure moments supervising the renovating of his 'country estate,' though he is living in town until his wife and daughter return."[11]

It was just over two months after the Jacksons moved into Hickory Hill that the Japanese attacked Pearl Harbor on December 7, 1941. The United States declared war against Japan and life changed for everyone, but it did not stop. The Jacksons involved themselves in the McLean community. They joined St. John's Episcopal Church which had relocated in 1917 from Langley to a site on Chain Bridge Road. Many items, such as sugar and gasoline, were rationed. To save on gasoline the justice often arrived at church via horse and buggy[12] and they both car pooled whenever possible. Residents in the greater Washington Metropolitan area were concerned about an air attack upon the nation's capital city. Because McLean was adjacent to the nation's capital, any aircraft flying overhead was of concern. Irene, as most of the area women, volunteered as an airplane spotter. She took a class with other women[13] and did volunteer duty at the McLean Volunteer Fire Station on Chain Bridge Road.

Newspapers were delivered by paper boys. While riding bicycles they tossed a rolled-up paper in the subscriber's driveway. As young teenagers, Philip Graves and Ray Watt covered the Langley area, which included Hickory Hill. Graves delivered the *Evening Star* and Watt delivered the *Washington Post*. It was also the job of the paper boy to collect the money each month. Both Graves and Watt would go together for the Hickory Hill collection. If home, Jackson would go out of his way to spend time with them. At Christmas time, he would invite them in for cookies and cocoa.[14] Hickory Hill was the site for the marriage of the Jackson's daughter, Mary Margaret, to Dr. Thomas Loftus, Jr. of Philadelphia, on November 20, 1943. The wedding was a simple ceremony that included a small intimate group, mainly consisting of the immediate families. The bride was attended by her close friend, Jean Wallace, the daughter of Vice President Henry Wallace and his wife Ilo. The newlywed couple moved to New York City, where Loftus was a resident physician in psychiatry at the New York Hospital[15] and Mary was involved in psychology related work at Bellview, a nearby hospital.[16]

Jackson had served four terms (one year each) as an associate justice when Roosevelt died suddenly in Warm Springs, Georgia, on April 12, 1945. At that time World War II was drawing to a close and Allied discussions were underway to prosecute captured high ranking Nazi leaders as war criminals. Rather than have each country separately try such surviving Nazi offenders for their war crimes, the discussions centered around proposals for an International Military Tribunal where a court of law would judge the guilt or innocence concerning the atrocities and war offenses of major Nazi figures. Such an international trial was unprecedented and, if held, it would be the first of its kind.

Roosevelt favored holding such legal proceedings, but not all the Allied nations were in agreement. As the newly sworn in President, Harry Truman concurred with Roosevelt's view and quickly designated Jackson on May 2, 1945, to represent the United States as the Chief Council in the proposed military tribunal.[17] Accepting the position meant that Jackson had to take a year's leave of absence from the bench of the Supreme Court beginning with the October, 1945 term. This left the Court with just eight justices to decide a ruling, allowing a potential for split decisions.

Jackson spent the summer of 1945 in London working to reach an agreement between the American, British, French and Russian governments to hold the principal high ranking Nazi figures individually accountable for their war crimes and lawfully try them before an International Military Tribunal. It was an enormously complex process of international diplomacy that would bring together four different systems of law. The agreement reached on August 8, 1945, became known as the London Charter. It was the legal basis for the trial that took place in the Palace of Justice before the International Military Tribunal beginning on November 20, 1945, in Nuremburg, Germany. Jackson gave the opening address for the prosecution the following day in a speech that lasted several hours. Extracts from the text of his opening remarks to the International Military Tribunal are as follows:

> "The privilege of opening the first trial in history for crimes against the peace of the world imposes a grave responsibility. The wrongs which we seek to condemn and punish have been so calculated, so malignant, and so devastating, that civilization cannot tolerate their being ignored, because it cannot survive their being repeated. That four great nations, flushed with victory and stung with injury stay the hand of vengeance and voluntarily submit their captive enemies to the judgment of the law is one of the most significant tributes that Power has ever paid to reason....

> What makes this inquest significant is that these prisoners represent sinister influences that will lurk in the world long after their bodies have returned to dust. We will show them to be living symbols of racial hatreds, of terrorism and violence, and of the arrogance and cruelty of power. They are symbols of fierce nationalisms and of militarism, of intrigue and mar-making which have embroiled Europe generation after generation, crushing its manhood, destroying its homes and impoverishing its life....

> Unfortunately, the nature of these crimes is such that both prosecution and judgment must be by victor nations over vanquished foes. The world-wide scope of the aggressions carried out by these men has left but few real neutrals. Wither the victors must judge the vanquished or we must leave the defeated to judge themselves. After the first World War, we learned the futility of the latter course....

> The case as presented by the United States will be concerned with the brains and authority back of all the crimes. These defendants were men of a station and rank which

does not soil its own hands with blood. They were men who know how to use lesser folks as tools. We want to reach the planners and designers, the inciters and leaders without whose evil architecture the world would not have been for so long scourged with the violence and lawlessness, and wracked with the agonies and convulsions of this terrible war....

In general, our case will disclose these defendants all uniting at some time with the Nazi party in a plan which they well knew could be accomplished only by an outbreak of war in Europe. Their seizure of the German state, their subjugation of the German people, their terrorism and extermination of dissident elements, their planning and waging of war, their calculated and planned ruthlessness in the conduct of warfare, their deliberate and planned criminally toward conquered peoples – all these are ends for which they acted in concert....

What we charge against these defendants is not those arrogances and pretensions which frequently accompany the intermingling of difficult peoples and which are likely, despite the honest efforts of government, to produce regrettable crimes and convulsions. It is my purpose to show a plan and design, to which all Nazis were fanatically committed to annihilate all Jewish people....

The persecution of the Jews was a continuous and deliberate policy. It was a policy directed against the Jews themselves. Anti-Semitism was promoted to divide and embitter the democratic peoples and to soften their resistance to the Nazi aggression.... History does not record a crime ever perpetrated against so many victims or one ever carried out with such calculated cruelty....

Determination to destroy the Jews was a binding force which at all times cemented the elements of this conspiracy. On many internal policies there were differences among the defendants. But there is not one of them who has not echoed the rallying cry of Nazism – "Deutschland erwache, Juda verrecke!" (Germany awake, Jewry perish!)....

The charter recognizes that one who has committed criminal acts may not take refuge in superior orders nor in the doctrine that his crimes were acts of States. These twin principles working together have heretofore resulted in immunity for practically everyone considered in the really great crimes against peace and mankind. Those in the lower ranks were protected against liability by the orders of their superiors. The superiors were protected because their orders were called acts of State. Under the charter, no defense Based on either of these doctrines can be entertained. Modern civilization puts unlimited weapons of destruction in the hands of men. It cannot tolerate so vast an area of legal irresponsibility....

But none of these men before you acted in minor parts. Each of them was entrusted with broad discretion and exercised great power. Their responsibility is correspondingly great and may not be shifted to that fictional being, "the State," which cannot be produced for trial, cannot plead, cannot testify and cannot be sentenced....

No charity can disguise the fact that the forces which these defendants represent, the forces that would advantage and delight in their acquittal, are the darkest and most sinister forces in society – dictatorship and oppression, malevolence and passion, militarism and lawlessness....These are the things that stand in the dock shoulder to shoulder with the prisoners. The real complaining party at your bar is civilization."[18]

The accused were the first war leaders of a defeated nation to be prosecuted in the name of the law, while also affording them the opportunity to plead for their innocence in the name of the law. There were 24 defendants, but only 22 were actually tried: Robert

Ley committed suicide while in prison before the hearings began and Gustav Krupt was rendered mentally incompetent to stand trial. One of the defendants, Martin Bormann was tried *in absentia*. Adolf Hitler, Heinrich Himmler, and Joseph Goebbels were not tried because they had committed suicide earlier. Each of the Nazi leaders was selected because he was a principal figure that represented a sector of power within the Third Reich: military, business, or political. Jackson personally cross-examined three of the defendants: Hermann Goering,[19] Albert Speer, and Hjalmar Schacht. The verdict imposed on 19 of the 22 defendants was guilty: 12 were sentenced to death, seven received prison sentences, and three were acquitted.[20]

The trial lasted much longer than everyone had anticipated. Jackson spent his year-plus in Europe without his wife who remained at Hickory Hill. During this time he became a grandfather for the first time. The Jacksons' daughter Mary gave birth to a son, Thomas Loftus III, in March of 1946. She spent a portion of her pregnancy with her mother at Hickory Hill confined with child bed fever while her husband was away serving the Navy as a general medical doctor in the Pacific region.[21] Jackson returned home in September of 1946 in time to return to the October, 1946 term of the Supreme Court.

Unfortunately, in 1949 the Loftus marriage ended in divorce. Mary returned to McLean to live in Walter Heights on Buchanan Street not far from Hickory Hill where she taught modern dance. Her two children, Thomas and William, attended both the Langley and Franklin Sherman Schools. On September 28, 1952, Mary married a lawyer, G. Bowdoin Craighill, in McLean's St John's Episcopal Church where the family worshiped. Craighill had served as a Naval officer in the Pacific theater during the War and was awarded the Silver Star.[22] The newlyweds moved into a home on Langley Lane, but in 1955 relocated to a residence on Waverly Way, formerly occupied by Henry and Bertha Shonerd and very near Hickory Hill.[23] The house was enlarged to include a dance studio and from there an exciting career as a modern dance instructor unfolded for Mary, having many McLean youth as her first students.[24]

A few months after the Supreme Court handed down its unanimous 1954 desegregation decision known as *Brown vs. Board of Education*, Jackson suffered a fatal heart attack on October 11, 1954. Services in Washington were held on October 13, 1954, at the National Cathedral, where more than 1000 people came to pay their respects.[25] Jackson's body was taken to Jamestown where he lay in state in St. Luke's Episcopal Church, prior to his burial in Frewsburg, just a few miles away.[26] Jackson's will left Hickory Hill in trust to his widow Irene. An appraisal of the estate was completed in February of 1955 by five appraisers appointed by the Circuit Court of Fairfax County. Two of the appointees, Verlin Smith and James Byrnes, appraised Hickory Hill at $86,000.[27] Irene remained living at Hickory Hill alone through the winter following her husband's death, but in the spring of 1955 she asked that the trustees, her son William and son-in-law Bowdoin, put the house up for sale. Hickory Hill was sold on October 15, 1955, to Senator John and Jacqueline Kennedy for $125,000.[28] Irene vacated Hickory Hill in October of 1955, a year after her husband's death, and moved into an apartment in Washington D. C.

Although Robert H. Jackson did not graduate from law school, he practiced law in the state of New York. His career dramatically advanced in 1938 when he became the United States Solicitor General. In 1940 he was selected to serve as the United States Attorney General, and in 1941 he was appointed to serve as an Associate Justice on United States Supreme Court.       (Library of Congress)

Attorney General Jackson is shown addressing the Senate Judiciary Committee concerning the Judicial Procedures Reform Bill of 1937, which came to be known as President Roosevelt's "court-packing plan." The bill ultimately failed.

(Library of Congress)

On June 2, 1937, during his tenure as Assistant Attorney General, Jackson appeared before the Senate and House Labor Committee in support of the Black-Connery Wage and Hour bill, which sought to establish a minimum wage and maximum workweek of 30 hours. Standing left to right are Representative William Connery, Jackson and Senator Hugo Black.

(Library of Congress)

Except for his leave of absence to prosecute Nazi war criminals at Nuremberg, Jackson served as an Associate Justice on the United States Supreme Court beginning in October of 1941 until his sudden death in 1954. He is shown wearing his justice attire shortly after being appointed to the court by President Franklin Roosevelt.   (Robert H. Jackson Center)

Shown above is President Franklin Roosevelt (seated), Mary Jackson (second from left) Irene Jackson (in white), and Robert Jackson at Jackson's 1941 swearing in ceremonies at the White House after being appointed to the United States Supreme Court. The bottom photo shows President Harry Truman with Jackson in 1945 discussing Jackson's duties as the leading United States representative to the International Military Tribunal where a court of law would hold leading Nazi figures individually accountable for their war crimes during World War II.

(Top: Library of Congress) (Bottom: Robert H. Jackson Center)

This photo of Hickory Hill was taken during early summer of 1942. A screened-in porch, once to the left of the house, is hidden by bushes. The lower picture shows Justice Jackson in the vegetable garden located in back of the house.

(Top: *House & Garden*)   (Bottom: John Q Barrett)

Justice Jackson is shown unveiling the family buggy at Hickory Hill. During World War II gasoline was rationed. To save on gasoline, he often arrived for Sunday services at St. John's Episcopal Church via horse and buggy.

(*House & Garden*)

The Jacksons enjoyed the country-side and horseback riding. Justice Jackson is pictured feeding apples to Renee, one of their horses.

(*House & Garden*)

Irene Jackson is shown above with the Jackson's dog
Pepper. She is standing below beside her kitchen stove
canning vegetables at Hickory Hill.

(Top: *House & Garden*)    (Bottom: John Q Barrett)

Supreme Court Justice Jackson was the chief United States Prosecutor at the International Nuremberg Trial, held for the purpose of dealing with Nazi war criminals and their war crimes against humanity. He is pictured above at the podium in 1945 giving opening remarks for the trial. The lower photo shows Jackson and Assistant Soviet Prosecutor General Uri Pokrovski on October 4, 1946, listening to a defense summation.

(Both: Robert H. Jackson Center © Raymond D'Addario)

# CHAPTER 10
## The John and Jacqueline Kennedy Residency

John Fitzgerald Kennedy was a first term senator from Massachusetts at the time he and his wife Jacqueline Bouvier purchased the 5.711 acre Hickory Hill estate; in 1960 he was elected the 35th President of the United States. Kennedy (known as JFK) graduated from Connecticut's Choate School in 1935, followed by Harvard in 1940 where he received his Bachelor of Science *cum laude* in international affairs. He joined the U.S. Naval Reserves during World War II and, in 1943, he was assigned to Motor Torpedo Squadron TWO. During the night of August 1-2 of that year Lieutenant Kennedy was in command of PT-109 when it was rammed and cut in half by the Japanese destroyer *Amagiri*.[1] Two of his men were immediately killed. Kennedy and the other ten survivors did not surrender, but managed to swim to an island three miles away. JFK towed a badly burned man through the water and then to a second island from where everyone was rescued. Kennedy was later awarded the Navy and Marine Corps Medal for heroism and the Purple Heart for injuries. After the War's end, Kennedy entered politics and, in 1947, was elected to represent Massachusetts in the House of Representatives.

Jackie, as she was known, was already familiar with the Langley/McLean area. One of her childhood homes was the nearby 47 acre Merrywood estate, where her mother, Janet Bouvier and step-father, Hugh Auchincloss, resided. Merrywood was located on Chain Bridge Road overlooking the Potomac River, not far from the Chain Bridge and no more than a mile from Hickory Hill.[2] Jackie spent three years at The Holton-Arms School and her high school days (1944-1947) at Miss Porter's School in Connecticut. She attended Vassar College for two years and went on to spend her junior year in France at the University of Grenoble and The Sorbonne in Paris. After returning to the United States she transferred to George Washington University where she graduated with a Bachelor of Arts degree in French literature and then was hired by the *Washington Times-Herald* as an "Inquiring Camera Girl." Jackie met her future husband in 1952 while he was still a congressman: that same year, he was elected to the Senate. They married the following year and, after honeymooning in Acapulco, the Kennedys settled into a residence in Georgetown.

As they were planning to begin a family, the Kennedys felt a larger house with more space was essential. The Jackson's white brick, Georgian style Hickory Hill home in rural Virginia was an easy trip to Capitol Hill and fulfilled their desires. After moving in, the senator wrote his Pulitzer Prize winning book *Profiles in Courage* while recovering from back surgery, and his wife began to plan and decorate a nursery for their anticipated first child. Unfortunately, things did not go as desired. Jackie suffered a miscarriage. This was followed on August 23, 1956, by a stillborn daughter, Arabella, whose birth occurred a week after the 1956 Chicago Democratic Convention at which her husband was almost selected to be on the ticket with Adlai Stevenson as the vice-presidential candidate. Jackie's disappointment at the loss of her daughter was great. She no longer wanted to live at Hickory Hill, and so, the couple moved back to Georgetown. Kennedy sold Hickory Hill to his parents, Joseph and Rose Kennedy, on January 2, 1957.[3] However, the grounds of Hickory Hill had once again diminished in size, but only slightly: on June 26, 1956, the Kennedys sold 3,457 square feet to their neighbor Sam Neel.[4] One of Kennedy's younger brothers, Robert, his wife Ethel, and their five children at that time, moved into Hickory Hill, leasing the property from the elder Kennedys.

While living at Hickory Hill, Senator Kennedy became involved with a proposal by the Virginia State Highway Department that called for widening a portion of Chain Bridge Road (Route 123) into a four-lane divided highway. The expansion was recommended in order to accommodate the increase in vehicular traffic that would be generated when the CIA relocated nearly 10,000 employees to its new headquarters at Langley in 1961. At that time, the two-lane Chain Bridge Road began just above the Chain Bridge on the Virginia side of the Potomac River. Its course proceeded through Langley, passed in front of Hickory Hill, and progressed through McLean as it wound in a southwesterly direction through Fairfax County to end at the Occoquan River. The Langley Ordinary, Hickory Hill, Ballantrae, Salona and the village of McLean were threatened by such a widening, but it went without question that the hamlet of Langley would lose its historical identity and appearance.

Homeowners along the route strongly objected to any widening of Chain Bridge Road because it would take land away from their property and bring a stream of vehicular traffic past their estate-like homes. However, other outraged citizens also raised their voices claiming this was the beginning of urbanization and looked upon the coming of the CIA as taking away the historic and rural atmosphere of the Langley area. Neel, whose property was adjacent to Hickory Hill, and Richard McAllister Smith, founder of the *McLean Providence Journal* headed up the citizen opposition. Along with the assistance of Senator Kennedy and other area residents, the Virginia State Highway Department was convinced that it should abolish its original plan and opt for a design that diverted the wider highway away from Langley and also McLean. And so, instead of following the path of the existing road, a four-lane divided highway was created. It ran in back of Hickory Hill and stretched from the George Washington Memorial Parkway to Anderson Road, using portions of the existing Chain Bridge Road. The new divided highway opened in 1962, leaving Langley and McLean undamaged. Hickory Hill remained untouched, but the new highway sliced through the Vernon Palmer farm (now Evermay), it divided the back of Mortimer Lebowitz's property (once owned by Louis Mackall), and it separated the front of the Ballantrae estate. Three acres were taken from Salona's frontage. This new thoroughfare, a by-pass for both Langley and McLean, was named Dolley Madison Boulevard:

> "President John F. Kennedy, a McLean resident shortly after becoming junior Senator from Massachusetts, played a leading role in determining the route of the future Dolley Madison Boulevard. Sen. Kennedy and the late Richard M. Smith, founder of the weekly McLean Providence Journal, were among those credited with persuading State highway authorities to pursue a route across largely open fields rather than widen Chain Bridge Road and destroy one of the most beautiful streets in McLean.
>
> President Kennedy had purchased the Hickory Hill home and estate from the widow of Justice Robert Jackson in 1955. After his unsuccessful bid for the Democratic vice presidential nomination in 1956, he transferred Hickory Hill to his brother, Robert, whose family still lives there."[5]

The photo shows the Hugh Dudley Auchincloss family ca.1946. A future First Lady Jacqueline Bouvier sits in the top back row. To her left is Hugh D. "Yusha" Auchincloss III. Jackie's sister Caroline Lee Bouvier is directly in front of her, followed by Nina Auchincloss to her left. Tommy Auchincloss is in the middle. In the front row is Janet Bouvier Auchincloss holding baby Janet, and Hugh D. Auchincloss.

(JFK Presidential Library)

Senator John and Jacqueline Bouvier Kennedy were married September 12, 1953. They are shown slicing their wedding cake during their Rhode Island reception held at the Auchincloss estate known as Hammersmith Farm.

(JFK Presidential Library)

The above photo shows Senator John and Jackie Kennedy enjoying the sunshine with younger relatives on the back patio at Hickory Hill. The lower picture depicts Senator Kennedy at a book signing for his Pulitzer Prize winning book *Profiles in Courage*.

(Top: Douglas Jones for *Look Magazine*)
(Bottom: JFK Library, Photographer unknown. Book cover: Harper and Bros.)

# CHAPTER 11
## The Robert and Ethel Kennedy Residency

Up until this time, Hickory Hill was basically a magnificent white brick Georgian style home, situated near the nation's capital city, in the countryside of McLean/Langley, Virginia. But after the Robert Kennedy family moved into the house, Hickory Hill suddenly became headlines in the national news. The youthful energy of the charismatic, athletic Kennedy clan put an imprint on the estate simply by the way they lived. The home was decorated somewhat formally with antiques, historic pieces and wonderful works of art, but done in a comfortable manner for easy living. The family of Robert (Bobby) and Ethel Skakel Kennedy was large and continually growing, so there was constant activity throughout the house and grounds. The house was large, but not large enough to accommodate everyone. In 1963 Ethel oversaw renovation and the construction of a north wing addition to the house. The screened porch was demolished to make room for a patio, a formal drawing room, a new living room, a second floor master bedroom suite, and additional bedrooms for the children. When finished, Hickory Hill had ten bathrooms (seven of which were full size), seven fireplaces and 13 bedrooms.[1] The surrounding grounds were turned into a recreational country club style setting which, besides the two existing sheds and stables for horses and ponies, now included a tennis court, an Olympic sized swimming pool, a children's pool and a pool house that included a kitchen with his and hers bathrooms.[2] A reptile house was built in the basement as a birthday present for Bobby, Jr.[3]

Overnight Hickory Hill became a household word and, in a sense, the Kennedys put McLean "on the map." The red front door became a McLean landmark. Just say the name and a vision of lots of adults and Kennedy children playing touch football comes to mind. They surrounded themselves with accomplished people from all walks of life; there was always a steady stream of friends, colleagues and dignitaries at the house. Theirs was an active life-style. From the very beginning of their residency there was constant activity whether it was in the form of tennis matches, touch football games, political events, fundraisers for charitable causes, or entertaining heads of state and other government officials. The size of the crowd did not seem to matter. It was a menagerie of children and animals that roamed freely. There was an aspect of pandemonium to the place. There were many pets for the children that over time included such animals as dogs, lambs, ponies, a seal, a honey bear, falcons, and snakes. Often social events turned into fraternity style parties and guests were known to have wound up, fully-clothed, in the swimming pool.[4] This was offset by intellectual stimulus in the form of the Hickory Hill seminars organized by Arthur Schlesinger, where guests would listen to leading scholars of the day and discuss a variety of topics over food and drink.[5]

When the Kennedys moved into Hickory Hill the surrounding landscape was still rural. One of the ways area residents, including Bobby, enjoyed country life was by riding their horses in and around McLean. But once the CIA made the decision to relocate to McLean, things changed. Trees were felled and land was cleared as old roads were widened and new roads were built to accommodate the increase in vehicular traffic. Many of the old riding trails were bulldozed into oblivion for these highways and for new homes that were being built in mushrooming subdivisions. There was little space left for riding. The Kennedys transported their horses and ponies between McLean and Hyannis Port, but, without convenient places to ride, they became too costly to maintain and were eventually phased out at Hickory Hill.[6]

Beginning in 1958, an annual spring Children's Pet Show was held on the grounds of Hickory Hill to raise funds for charity. Neighbors and friends were invited to bring their pets, but they had to have purchased a ticket in advance. Hundreds of children and their parents turned out for the event, bringing every pet imaginable. Many celebrities were present. Art Buchwald presided as the ringmaster wearing an oversized red morning coat, high leather boots and black top hat. Anything a child considered to be a pet was judged (even pet rocks) and, no matter what, every child received a prize. Among the various animals that children brought were cats, dogs, snakes, lizards, caterpillars, parrots, rabbits, raccoons, gerbils, geese, chickens, fish and turtles. In 1968 Pennebaker and Hegedus Films produced a documentary of the event which was narrated by George Plimpton.[7] In 1978 the major attraction was a three ton Indian elephant from the Ringling Brothers and Barnum & Bailey Circus which broke lose after being spooked by a barking dog. The elephant, named Suzie, broke through the roped off show ring sending judges and pet-clutching children scrambling for safety. Suzie broke through a neighbor's fence, but was secured shortly thereafter.[8] The McLean Volunteer Fire Department was always on hand for safety and to provide rides for the children on their hook-and-ladder truck. However, one year the rides were briefly halted because two firemen had to climb a tree and rescue a Siamese cat named Tangerine that had gotten away from its owner.[9] In addition, there was food and a variety of entertainment over the years for children: this included pony rides, puppet shows, treasure hunts, celebrity tennis and an obstacle course conducted by several Washington Redskins. Buckwald, in his memoirs of the Kennedys, briefly described the pet show:

"They have a pet show every year. And it's a pretty wild affair where everybody brings an animal, and we have prizes for the best, longest tail, the shortest tail, longest nose, the shortest nose. And the Kennedys, naturally, always had thousands of pets in the cellar of the house so that no matter what you had, there was a pet for it. And the Kennedys always wanted to win first prize. This is something about the Kennedys, they will never settle for a second-prize ribbon. So I was a judge and so there was a tremendous amount of pressure being put on me by Ethel.... It's kidding on the square. They pretend they're kidding, but they're not kidding. And it is kind of unfair to the rest of the kids when the Kennedys came in with a hawk or with some animal that Bobby Kennedy, Jr., picked up in Africa, but we took care of them very well. I once gave them third prize, and I think that it was the worst thing I ever did to them.

At the pet show, the most famous anecdote about Bobby that I can remember.... Bobby supposedly had a great deal of courage and Brumus, who played a big role in Bobby's life--Brumus was the big Lapland black dog whom everyone hated. I mean there was nobody who had a nice thing to say about Brumus, and Bobby loved Brumus. After the show, people just sit on the lawn and they picnic there. And Bobby and I were sitting, relaxed on the stoop, watching everybody having a nice time and everything, and suddenly Brumus wandered down. And there were these two ladies that were, I guess, around sixty each, sitting eating their lunch. Suddenly Brumus lifted his leg and peed on one of them. Well, she didn't see him and I guess it took about a minute for this to soak through. Bobby went white and he ran into the house. So when it came to a profile of courage in regards to Brumus, he was a coward."[10]

On January 20, 1961, Senator John Fitzgerald Kennedy was sworn in as the 35th President of the United States by Chief Justice Earl Warren. The new president immediately appointed the oldest of his younger brothers and campaign manager, Bobby, to the position of Attorney General of the United States. During his brief term in office, the president dealt with such matters as the Bay of Pigs Invasion, the Cuban Missile Crisis, the building of the Berlin Wall, the African-American Civil Rights Movement, Project Apollo and the early stages of the Vietnam War. Bobby became a close advisor to the president and was involved in many foreign policy discussions. As attorney general, he campaigned relentlessly against organized crime and devoted energy to civil rights for all Americans.

Bobby's campaign against organized crime stemmed from his role as committee counsel to the Senate Rackets Committee that investigated corrupt trade unions, particularly the International Brotherhood of Teamsters. The hearings began in 1957 and lasted over two years. During that time Bobby furiously went after Jimmy Hoffa, the Teamsters president, and interrogated him relentlessly. Kennedy thought Hoffa was corrupt and removing him from power would make the Teamsters a better union. A long bitter feud developed between the two men that gained intensity when Bobby was appointed attorney general and continued until Bobby's untimely death in 1968. The two men hated each other. *Look Magazine* published an article in March of 1964 relating a story, offered by Edward Grady Partin, suggesting that persons within the Teamsters organization had earlier considered assassinating Kennedy. Partin, who had been the business manager for Teamsters Local 5 in Baton Rouge, Louisiana, for several years, was being held on a kidnapping charge in the East Baton Rouge Parish Building. Pardin revealed his story on September 29, 1962, to the warden, Captain Thomas Edwards, who immediately contacted William (Billy) Daniels, an assistant to District Attorney Sargent Pitcher. The story Partin related to Pitcher suggested a plot which was to either plant plastic explosives at the Hickory Hill house or toss explosives into Bobby's open convertible as he was driving about town:

> "Alone with Daniels, Partin poured out the story. A few weeks earlier, when he had been in Washington at the International Teamsters headquarters, Partin said he was called into a Teamster office, and was asked about obtaining plastic explosives for the assassination of the Attorney General. 'Something has to be done about that little s.o.b., Bobby Kennedy,' Partin quoted a Teamster official as saying. 'He'll be an easy target, always driving around Washington in that convertible with that big black dog. All we need is some plastic explosives tossed in with him, and that will finish him off.'
>
> Partin said he was told that some thought was also being given to using the plastic explosives on the Kennedy home at McLean, Va. A plastic bomb planted at the Kennedy home would also endanger the Kennedy children and Partin has small children of his own....[11]

*Brown vs. Board of Education* became the law of the land in 1958. Not all of the states were in compliance and Bobby was determined to enforce it. In September of 1962 Kennedy ordered United States Marshalls and troops to Oxford, Mississippi to make certain that James Meredith was admitted to the University of Mississippi.[12] He further fought discrimination through his commitment to securing equal voting rights for African Americans. The landmark Civil Rights Act of 1964 passed eight months after President Kennedy was assassinated. Bobby had retired as attorney general to run for the United States Senate from the state of New York, where he planned to continue his fight to eliminate discrimination.

It was during the early winter of 1962 that the daughter of the Russian Premier Nikita Khrushchev, Rada Khrushchev and her husband Alexei Adzhubei, had a whirlwind three-day stay in Washington between trips to Mexico, Canada and Brazil.[13] This was during the years of the Cold War when relations between the United States and Russia were strained. A small intimate luncheon was held at the White House on January 30,[14] which was followed the next day with a somewhat informal luncheon at Hickory Hill. The meal consisted of broiled grapefruit, roast beef with potatoes, peas, squash and a chocolate roll covered with chocolate sauce for dessert. The Kennedy children then took the guests on a tour of the grounds, including the animals. Later, at the State Department, Rada remarked that it would be a good idea for Russian women to see American homes:

> "…Mrs. Adzhubei and her husband went to the 6-acre estate of Attorney General and Mrs. Robert F. Kennedy in McLean. The Kennedys' youngsters ate their lunch early, and so they were ready to take their visitors on a tour of the stables and grounds of 'Hickory Hill.'
>
> Rada Adzhubel's eyes lighted up as she spoke of the Kennedy youngsters and their pets. A horsewoman herself, she was especially interested in having the Attorney General's children show her their ponies. She admired their ducks and goats and petted their dogs too.
>
> She said she enjoyed being in an American home and the delicious, but simple, lunch of broiled grapefruit, roast beef with potatoes, peas and squash, with a chocolate roll with chocolate sauce for dessert.
>
> 'I think it would be a good idea for Russian women to see American homes,' she said later at the State Department."[15]

Ethel and Bobby were at Hickory Hill the afternoon of November 22, 1963, when President Kennedy was assassinated while part of a motorcade in Dallas, Texas. Bobby was having lunch by the swimming pool when he received a phone call from J. Edgar Hoover that his brother had been shot. Twenty minutes later Hoover phoned again to say that the president had died.[16] Bobby did not leave Hickory Hill at that time, but instead walked the grounds in reflective thought with two of his dogs, Brumus and Rusty. The Secret Service, Federal Marshalls, Fairfax County Police and reporters surrounded the estate in belief that the shooting was part of a larger conspiracy and Bobby might be the next target. A McLean resident and Fairfax County police officer, Gary Heath, later remarked on the event:

> "One of the interesting things that happened in my early career with Fairfax County was the assassination of President John Kennedy. This happened while I was still assigned to the Special Investigation Squad at headquarters doing plain clothes surveillance work. Because I lived in McLean I was sent over to Hickory Hill, in uniform. At that time

Hickory Hill was the home of Robert Kennedy, Attorney General and brother to the President. There was little information at first, and many thought that the shooting might be part of a larger conspiracy. The police department told me to put my uniform on and assigned me to security at Hickory Hill in McLean. There were also lots of FBI, Secret Service, and reporters there. It was mass confusion. I had orders not to let anyone in the driveway. It took awhile to get some order. Nobody knew what was going on at first. It was understandable. I took my orders from Fairfax County. At one point, I was directing traffic. The Holliday family across the street from Hickory Hill generously set up a card table with coffee and sandwiches.

I was there for three days; we couldn't leave. We couldn't spare anybody to go get food. To use a bathroom, we had to drive back to McLean to the firehouse on Chain Bridge Road. There was a Pizza Supreme in McLean at that time. The owner was a retired Marine sergeant. He sent down boxes and boxes of sandwiches to feed us. Later the Kennedy family sent me, and some others, a very nice note acknowledging our expression of sympathy and service." [17]

Shortly after his brother's death, Kennedy began exploring the possibility of running against the Republican incumbent, Senator Kenneth Keating, for the United States Senate from the state of New York. A ca.1830 Dutch colonial style farmhouse, with an exorbitant number of rooms, was leased from fashion designer Philip Hulitar in Glen Cove on Long Island for two years. [18] The plan was to spend time at both residences, so that the school schedules of their seven children at that time would not be disrupted. Of course, the Republicans throughout the campaign hammered away that he was riding his brother's coattails and was a carpetbagger from Massachusetts who established a residency in New York simply to run for office. It was also pointed out that he lived in Virginia, but maintained his voting address in Massachusetts. During their residency at Hickory Hill, Bobby and Ethel continued to lease from the older Kennedys. It wasn't until January 8, 1965, two months after Kennedy won the New York senate election, that Ethel purchased the Hickory Hill estate from Bobby's parents, Joseph and Rose Kennedy.[19]

Kennedy was a well-qualified challenger for the senate position. He understood politics, the operations of government and had already gained national recognition of his own. After serving in the United States Navy, Kennedy graduated from Harvard College and received his law degree from the University of Virginia's School of Law in 1951. Following graduation, he briefly served on Senator Joseph McCarthy's Senate Committee on Unamerican Activities. He went on to become the chief council of the Senate Labor Rackets Committee from 1957-1959, where he challenged Hoffa about corruption within the union. He then published a book about corruption in organized labor titled *The Enemy Within*. During his tenure as attorney general he became nationally known for supporting African American civil rights. Bobby had been the campaign manager for his brother, John, during the 1960 presidential election, served as the chief White House adviser to the president during his brother's brief tenure in office and helped resolve the Cuban Missile Crisis.

From the lawn of Gracie Mansion, with New York's Mayor, Robert Wagner, at his side, 38 year old Kennedy announced his candidacy for the Senate on August 25, 1964. A little over one week later, on September 3, 1964, Kennedy resigned his government position as attorney general. He then went to the White House to officially acknowledge his resignation to President Lyndon Johnson.[20] *The Washington Post* reported on September 4, 1964, that Kennedy thought his greatest accomplishments while serving as attorney general were in the field of civil rights:

> "He said that in his 3 ½ years as Attorney General he got the greatest satisfaction in the field of civil rights. He said that the big problem ahead was not enforcement, but a conscientious effort by whites and Negroes to improve relations."[21]

This was also the year of the 36th presidential election with the Democratic ticket headed by President Johnson and Senator Hubert Humphrey. Kennedy handily defeated Keating, but the votes cast for him were far less than the Democratic landslide achieved by the Johnson/Humphrey slate. On that same date, November 3, 1964, Kennedy's younger brother, Edward ("Ted") was re-elected in Massachusetts, soundly defeating the Republican challenger, Howard Whitmore, Jr. This placed two Kennedy brothers in the Senate at the same time. Many felt that Bobby's election to represent New York in the senate was but a stepping stone for a 1968 presidential campaign. *The Washington Post* wrote on September 5, 1964, that "The battle between the Kennedy clan and the Johnson-Humphry forces will not be officially declared, but it has already started."

Earlier in 1964, a small group of local skiing enthusiasts organized the Ballantrae Ski Club with dues of $50 per year. Joseph Rosenbaum, the owner of Ballantrae Farm (formerly known as the Franklyon Farm), allowed the group to use a hill on the east side of his property to ski down to the newly created Dolley Madison Boulevard. The hill was approximately 450 feet in height. It was cleared, and a fence at the bottom on adjoining property was moved in order for the skiers to have a flat place for a runout. Trails were laid out, marking poles were appropriately placed and a rope tow was installed. Power was supplied by an old truck or jeep. The club took out a public liability insurance policy covering each of the members by name. There were even four flood lights. The use of sleds, toboggans and saucers were forbidden. By December of that year 16 families had signed up, including Ethel and Bobby Kennedy. During that same month there was enough snow for the skiing to begin and the ski tow began operating.[22]

During Bobby's senatorial days Ethel found herself enmeshed in a contentious Fairfax County lawsuit in which she was accused of being a horse thief and was sued for $30,000. The suit, At Law No. 14845, was filed on October 7, 1965.[23] It stemmed from an incident that took place two years earlier on October 8, 1963. Ethel, while riding horseback with several of her children across property located along Georgetown Pike (she had permission) came across a neglected, starving horse that was basically skin and bones. Upon returning home she instructed her groom, Richard Mayberry, to rescue the horse, a thoroughbred yearling named Pande, and lead it back to the barn at Hickory Hill in order to save its life and restore its health. This was done. The Animal Welfare League was contacted. After an approved agent, Dr. William Santoro, evaluated the obvious unhealthy condition of the horse, he agreed that Pande had been neglected and cruelly treated and, he assumed responsibility for the horse and its further care.[24] Pande's owner, Nicholas Zemo, was notified immediately of the circumstances. Zemo, a horse breeder, owned several other horses. He lived in Washington D.C. and leased the land, plus several other properties in the greater McLean area, for his horses. This was not the first time he had been admonished for not taking proper care of his animals. In August of 1962 the West Virginia Racing Commission suspended his license indefinitely "for abandoning and for failing to make arrangements for the proper care of his horses."[25] Unfortunately, in spite of all the assistance, Pande died five days after arriving at Hickory Hill.[26] The following month, Nicholas N. Zemo, was convicted of cruelty to seven horses after Judge William Plummer listened to Ethel's testimony. The judge described this as one of the clearest cases of cruelty by neglect that he had ever seen. He fined Zemo $250 and gave him a suspended six-month jail sentence.[27] Zemo waited nearly two years before filing for damages. The suit alleged that Mayberry stole Pande and took him to Hickory Hill and, upon request, Ethel refused to return the horse. A jury trial, consisting of 13 persons, took place on January 9, 1967, at the courthouse in Fairfax County. The following verdict was delivered by the jury and the case was dismissed.

"January 10, 1967
We the jury on the issue joined in the case
of Nicholas N. Zemo vs. Mrs. Robert F. Kennedy
find in favor of the defendant."[28]

The ink was barely dry from printing the results of the 1964 New York state senate election before reporters began speculating about the 1968 presidential election. As it turned out, Kennedy was a late entry into that contest and did not announce until March 16, 1968.[29] This was just a few days after the New Hampshire primary held on March 12, 1968, in which President Lyndon Johnson defeated Eugene McCarthy, a United States Senator from Minnesota, in a closely contested race.[30] Kennedy made his announcement from the same spot in the Senate Caucus Room where his brother, John, had declared his presidential candidacy on January 2, 1960.[31] He knew that it would not be easy to defeat the incumbent president, but the Vietnam War and race relations were creating deep divisions of opinion throughout the nation, offering him a strong "window of opportunity." Just two weeks after Kennedy's presidential announcement, President Johnson unexpectedly shocked the nation by declaring he would cease bombing North Vietnam in an attempt to deescalate the war and move toward peace: at the same time, he dropped out of the presidential race.[32] Vice President Humphrey then entered the contest. The 1968 Democratic presidential race now had three contestants, but it was too late for Humphrey to be on the primary ballot in many states; however, they did allow for a write-in candidate.

On June 4, 1968, Kennedy won the California primary with 46% of the vote to McCarthy's 42%.[33] This was a significant blow to McCarthy's campaign because all of the California Democratic delegates to the national Democratic convention would vote for Kennedy under California's "winner take all" rules. Around midnight that evening 42 year-old Kennedy addressed his supporters in a ballroom at the Ambassador Hotel in Los Angeles. After giving his victory speech and celebrating, Kennedy exited through a service area in the a.m. hours of June 5. In a crowded kitchen passageway Sirhan Sirhan, a Palestinian militant who disliked Kennedy because of his support for Israel, fired and shot Kennedy several times at close range with a .22 caliber revolver.[34] Five others were wounded in the attack: William Weisel of Washington, D. C. and Paul Schrade, Elizabeth

Evans, Ira Goldstein, and Irwin Stroll who all resided in the Los Angeles area.[35] Kennedy died the following morning, June 6, at the Good Samaritan Hospital in Los Angeles.[36]

Later that afternoon, the senator's body was flown to New York City, arriving at La Guardia Airport just before 9:00 p.m. Thousands lined the streets, sidewalks and bridges to pay their respect as the hearse carrying Kennedy's body made its way to St. Patrick's Cathedral.[37] The following day Kennedy lay in state in a flag draped closed coffin. A lengthy line of mourners, over 25 blocks long, waited in the hot humid weather to enter the cathedral and pay their respects. Over 2000 invited guests attended the requiem mass. Presiding at the funeral mass and representing Pope Paul VI, was Angelo Cardinal Dell'Acqua, the Pope's vicar for New York City and the District of Rome.[38] After the mass, Kennedy's body was taken by a 21 car funeral train to Washington D. C. Thousands of mourners lined the tracks along the entire route. At Elizabeth, New Jersey two bystanders were killed and six others were injured by a northbound express which rounded a curve at a high rate of speed and plowed into the crowd that had overflowed onto the tracks.[39] The arrival of the funeral train was delayed, so that it did not reach Union Station until 9:08 p.m., five hours later than originally scheduled.[40] A motorcade led the funeral procession to Arlington National Cemetery where, after a gravesite service that began at 10:30 p.m., Kennedy was laid to rest on a grassy hillside near the grave of his brother, John.[41] This was the only night-time burial in the cemetery's history. In addition to the service at St. Patrick's, other churches and synagogues throughout the nation offered a special service or prayers during their regular scheduled services throughout the day. St. Luke Catholic Church in McLean, Holy Trinity in Georgetown, and St. Francis Xavier in Hyannis Port, Massachusetts, three churches where the Kennedy family worshipped, held a requiem mass.

The days of Camelot skidded to a halt. Ethel, who was expecting again, suddenly found herself a widow with ten children: Kathleen (Townsend); Joseph 2nd; Robert, Jr.; David; Courtney (Hill); Michael; Kerry; Christopher; Max; Douglas. The Kennedy's eleventh child, a daughter Rory (Bailey), was born on December 12, 1968, six months after her father's death. Raising 11 children without the benefit of a husband is a difficult task no matter how much help one is able to obtain. These were not easy years. Bobby has been her best friend. Even though she kept an upbeat outward appearance, Ethel suffered greatly. As a Roman Catholic, she leaned heavily on her faith, seldom missing daily mass at St. Luke when in McLean. She has not remarried. Rumors often circulated linking her with various personalities, particularly Andy Williams, but nothing serious developed from any of the relationships. Negative publicity and tragedy stuck Ethel over and over again. There were scandals within the Skakel family and that of her brother-in-law Senator Ted Kennedy. Her nephew, John Kennedy, Jr., his wife and her sister, were killed in a plane crash. But the most severe pain involved her children. In 1973 her oldest son Joseph was driving a jeep with six other passengers on Nantucket Island. It overturned; a passenger, Pam Kelley, would never walk again.[42] Then in 1984 her son David was found dead in a Palm Beach hotel room due to a drug overdose,[43] and during the late afternoon of December 31, 1997, Michael died in a skiing accident in Aspen,

Colorado, after hitting a tree during a makeshift touch football game on the slopes.[44] This was followed in 2012 with the unexpected death of Mary, the wife of Bobby, Jr.

From the beginning, the Kennedys enjoyed their house and all the amenities the property and surrounding area had to offer. There was always a strong scene of energy about the place, combined with a mischievous sense of humor, which continued after Bobby's death. For instance, a small handmade sign was posted near the driveway in the front yard that read, "No trespassing: Violators will be eaten."[45] A bronze plaque was placed on a hearthstone stating, "N.O.N. Historical Marker --- On This Spot, February 1776, Absolutely Nothing Happened."[46] In the library was framed text that read, "Will the woman who left her 11 children at R.F.K. Stadium, please come and pick them up. They're beating the redskins 14 – 0."[47]

As the children married and went their own way, Ethel found herself an "empty nester" and the house was just too large for her. She put Hickory Hill up for sale in 2003 for a hefty $25,000,000.[48] It remained on the real estate market for several years and underwent several price reductions before the Hickory Hill Trust purchased it for Alan and Ashley Dabbiere in December of 2009 for $8,250,000;[49] the Dabbieres then undertook a near-total transformation of the house.

This picture of Hickory Hill was taken during the winter of 1965 and published in the *Northern Virginia Sun* newspaper. The stables are to the far right in the background.

(Bill Little: *Northern Virginia Sun*)

This is Hickory Hill as it looked in 2000. The front door was red. The stone walkway that led from the front steps connected with a semi-circular asphalt driveway. To the left is the yard urn that Justice Jackson requested be conveyed with the sale of the house.

(Carole Herrick)

This is a magnificent springtime view of Hickory Hill taken from its north side.
(The RFK Kennedy Family)

This photo, taken in 2007, is another view of Hickory Hill's north side. This was the wing that was enlarged in 1963 to include a formal drawing room, a new living room, a second floor master suite and additional bedrooms for the children. Of interest are the many air conditioning units in the various windows. (Quarterczar)

Senator John Kennedy is shown with his brother Robert at Hickory Hill. Senator Kennedy purchased Hickory Hill in 1955, but moved back to Georgetown two years later. He sold the estate to his father Joseph P. Kennedy (lower), former ambassador to the Court of St. James, under whose ownership it remained until Ethel Kennedy purchased it in 1965.

(Top: JFK Memorial Library)    (Bottom: Library of Congress)

The Robert Kennedy family sits for a photograph in 1957 on the back lawn of their newly purchased home known as Hickory Hill. The five children from left to right are Joe, age four; David, age one; Bobby, Jr., age three; Kathleen, age five; and baby Courtney sitting on her mother's lap.

(Paul Schutzer/Getty Images)

Senator John Kennedy is receiving a pass from his brother Bobby on the grounds in back of the house. The photograph was taken shortly after Ethel and Bobby moved to McLean.

(Paul Schutzer/Getty Images)

Ethel with her five children and three dogs is enjoying an afternoon at Hickory Hill via horse and cart shortly after settling into the house.          (The RFK Kennedy Family)

The spirit of the RFK Kennedy family was an outdoor athletic lifestyle which included the girls. Here Ethel is shown pointing out the finer points of kick ball to daughters Kathleen, Courtney and Kerry.

(The RFK Kennedy Family)

As busy as the Kennedys were, they always found time to spend time with their children. Here Bobby is enjoying an afternoon in Hickory Hill's backyard with Kathleen, Joe and Bobby, Jr. The north wing of the house had not yet been remodeled to accommodate a growing family.

(The RFK Kennedy Family)

Bobby, left, just confirmed reports that he will resign as Chief Council for the Senate Rackets Investigating Committee in order to take on a major position in his brother's campaign for President of the United States.  (Library of Congress)

The 64th Attorney General of the United States, Robert Kennedy, is shown testifying before a Senate subcommittee on crime in 1963. Kennedy served in this position from January 20, 1961, to September 3, 1964.  (Library of Congress)

The above picture shows, Alexei Adzhubei, his wife Rada Khrushchev, and Georgi Bolshakov with his wife standing outside Hickory Hill where they were luncheon guests on January 31, 1962. Rada was the daughter of Soviet Premier Nikita Khrushchev and Alexei was the editor-in-chief of the official Russian government newspaper *Izvestia*.                          (Library of Congress)

Standing in the White House Rose Garden after the 1963 special Conference on Civil Rights, are left to right Martin Luther King, Jr., leader of the Southern Christian Leadership Conference, Attorney General Robert Kennedy, Roy Wilkens, Executive Secretary for the National Association for the Advancement of Colored People, and Vice President Lyndon Johnson.                    (Library of Congress)

New York's mayor Robert Wagner raises the hand of Attorney General Robert F. Kennedy as RFK declares his candidacy for the U. S. Senate representing the state of New York.                                  (Library of Congress)

Senator Kennedy is shown at Hickory Hill during a 1968 presidential campaign strategy session. Pictured left to right are Kennedy, his brother-in-law Steven Smith and his younger brother Ted Kennedy.                                (Burt Glinn/Magum Photos)

This 1968 photo shows presidential candidate Robert Kennedy once again enjoying family football in the yard in back of the house. Of interest is the north wing enlargement which had not yet taken place in the football photo on page 116.                (Burt Glinn/Magnam Photos)

This 1968 photograph shows Bobby at Hickory Hill with his beloved dog Brumus and eight of his children shortly before going out on the presidential campaign trail.

(Burt Glinn/Magnum Photos)

The photo shows Kennedy, minutes before he was assassinated, addressing a crowd of supporters as he claimed victory in the June California Democratic primary for President of the United States. He left the room through a side door on his way to the ballroom where he was to give his acceptance speech, but was fatally shot by Sirhan Sirhan as he travelled down the pantry corridor. (Julian Wesser/Getty Images)

The above photo was taken during one of the Easter egg hunts at Hickory Hill. The lower photo shows Art Buckwald briefly resting with Ethel Kennedy at Hickory Hill's 21st Annual Pet Show held on May 19, 1979, to benefit the Runaway House.

(Top: The RFK Kennedy Family)    (Lower: Ron Galia/Getty Images)

# CHAPTER 12
## The Dabbiere Residency

Alan and Ashley Dabbiere arrived on the McLean scene in 2006 after spending two years sailing around the world on a yacht which was named after their daughter Constance. Alan, a technology entrepreneur, graduated from the University of Indiana where he majored in chemistry with plans on becoming a medical doctor. He decided that medicine was not for him and continued his studies at Indiana earning his M.B.A. After graduation he took a job with a consulting firm and, after four years, left to form Manhattan Associates, a supply-chain logistics firm based in Manhattan Beach, California. The company moved to Atlanta, Georgia shortly thereafter and went public on the NADAQ Exchange in 1998. While in Atlanta he met and married Ashley Bittman, a communications graduate of the University of Arizona who was working as a media executive with Meredith Corporation. Alan stepped off the board of Manhattan Associates and in 2003 the couple, along with Constance, set out on an adventurous journey to sail the world.[1]

After two years they decided to forgo living on the water. During this period they had added to their family with twin boys. They recognized that children require a permanent home and schooling: also, Alan was ready to start a new venture. They were drawn to the greater Washington Metropolitan area because it was rapidly turning into a technology center. They purchased a home in the Langley section of McLean, not too far from Hickory Hill, and took up residency.[2] Soon thereafter, Alan formed Air-Watch, a mobile device management company also headquartered in the Atlanta suburbs.[3] Hickory Hill was already listed for sale: it had been placed on the market during 2003 at a very steep asking price of $25,000,000.[4] It remained on the market for six years, with several price reductions, before the Dabbieres purchased it in 2009 for $8,200,000 through the Hickory Hill Trust.[5] The deed lists a colleague John Marshall as the grantor and head of the Hickory Hill Trust. The Dabbieres were especially pleased that they were able to purchase the property as opposed to a developer with visions of subdividing the land with McMansons. Shortly after purchasing the 5.631 acre piece of American history, the Hickory Hill Trust bought an adjoining 2.2238 acres located in back of the estate,[6] increasing the acreage to approximately eight acres.

Hickory Hill conjures pleasant memories to many of pet shows, Easter egg hunts, trick or treating and Kennedy family football, but the house had not been adequately maintained after RFK's death. Hickory Hill had aged and it showed. Significant repairs were necessary by the time it was placed on the real estate market and the house needed to be modernized to meet today's standards. For instance, there was no central air conditioning. The neighbors maintained they always knew when winter had ended and spring had arrived by the air conditioning units in many of the windows. There was no garage, the plumbing was antiquated, and the electrical system was outdated. The kitchen proved inadequate for today's lifestyle. It was more like a staff kitchen built in the 1950s that had a commercial/industrial feel to it. The house featured 12 mostly very small bedrooms, ten bathrooms, one-half bath and nine fireplaces.[7] Even though Hickory Hill is a significant historic property no one had ever placed it individually in the National

Register of Historic Places. However, it was added to the Virginia Landmarks Register, listed in Fairfax County's Inventory of Historic Sites, included in the Langley Fork National Register Historic District as a contributing property and in the Fairfax County Langley Fork Historic Overlay District as a historic property. The only one of these designations that provides any oversight and protection is the local county historic overlay district.[8] Once the community realized that Hickory Hill would be placed on the real estate market, many insisted that the house should be preserved as a museum, but many residents downplayed that idea insisting that the Langley area was not suitable for such a "tourist attraction." Many hardline historic preservationists did not want changes to the house or property, but their expectations were too high. The problems went beyond historic preservation. If a family was to reside at Hickory Hill, then the house had to be updated to fit today's lifestyle. The Dabbieres realized that if they wanted to continue with the history and longevity of the house, then the restoration repairs would be major and costly. They were wary and carefully assessed the situation before purchasing Hickory Hill.

Being passionate about history, the Dabbieres understood the extraordinary significance of the property and did everything possible to reduce the disturbance to the house. Before tackling the risk involved in a lengthy project, they met with historians, architects and engineers to go over the many challenges they faced because of past alterations to the original house. Since the house was included in the Fairfax County Langley Fork Historic Overlay District any alterations needed to be approved by Fairfax County's Architectural Review Board (ARB). This was a public hearing type process which resulted in the ARB approving large scale additions, but holding firm that it would not accept anything that would obscure the view deep into the property.[9] Then, in 2010, the Dabbieres began a monumental three year project to renovate the house, working with John Milner Architects, a well-known firm experienced in historic preservation and restoration construction.

A near total transformation of the house by local builders took place that ended in January of 2014. Through numerous photographs and videos, the Dabbieres meticulously documented and preserved what had been there previously. They did not disappoint. The result was a wonderful balance between the old and the new. It did not hurt that they had a high quality bias. The basic outside facade remained, even though the roof in the rear was partially raised to create a bigger guest room. As in the original house built by Walters, Virginia slate was used for the new roof. However, the entire interior underwent a complete change, taking the home back to the studs and rearranging the floorplan to better support the previous renovations. The basement was reconfigured to include a bedroom, kitchenette, an elevator, and a Hickory Hill historical room. A three story addition was built to the south side of the house that included a five car garage at the basement level. The pool house and tennis court remained, but the swimming pool itself had to be rebuilt and the mechanical apparatus had to be replaced. The tennis court was cracked and peeling and, so, it was resurfaced. The horse stables were turned into office space and Alan relocated his business from Elm Street in McLean into the building. The semi-circular driveway remained, connecting to Chain Bridge Road at both ends. It now includes a vehicular circle in the middle and the northern end remains closed unless there are large-scale events taking place at the house.[10]

In 2012 Ashley was diagnosed with a glioma-type brain tumor. She underwent surgery to remove as much of the tumor as possible. Unfortunately, removing all of this type of tumor is impossible and, so, she is monitored every three months. This is an illness that she will battle the remainder of her life. In May of 2015, with the support of the National Brain Tumor Society, the Dabbieres hosted their first big event, "The Grey Soiree," on the grounds of Hickory Hill. The gala was held to help raise the awareness and resources needed to find better treatments, and ultimately a cure, for brain tumors. It featured the entertainment of nine-time Grammy award winner Sheryl Crow and food and wine from Washington's top chefs. Besides the presence of many pioneers from the brain tumor community, a multitude of residents from McLean and other Northern Virginia municipalities turned out to support the cause. The inaugural "Grey Soiree" sold out: it raised more than $1,000,000.[11] The funds went to the National Brain Tumor Society, the largest nonprofit dedicated to finding better treatments and cures for brain tumors. Many causes have a color. For instance, breast cancer is pink. The word grey was a play on the grey matter in a person's brain.

The Dabbieres have hosted other large-scale events at Hickory Hill since the renovations were completed. They relish the history of the property. They recognize that their residence is a significant part of the area's heritage and that the importance of their house, its care and splendid legacy, is important to Virginia and the McLean community. Hickory Hill was purchased before developers acquired it and the Dabberies put the necessary funding into quality workmanship. The result is a residence far grander than before, but it continues Hickory Hill's legacy as a magnificent landmark for McLean.

Hickory Hill was first listed on the residential real estate market in 2003 at an asking price of $25,000,000. The price was lowered several times before the property was purchased on December 31, 2009. Both photos show an addition to the front yard not seen in previous pictures: this is the flag pole. The above photo was used in promoting the house by the listing agent at Washington Fine Properties, LLC.

(Top: Ted Gossett and Florence Meers)      (Bottom: The Dabbiere Family)

Hickory Hill was built atop a knoll facing Chain Bridge Road. This 1968 photo features the front and north side of the house after its 1963 addition. Of interest is the large tree near the front door. It is not seen in the other photos and appears to have stood where the flag pole was later placed.

(Fairfax County Department of Planning and Zoning)

Hickory Hill was built ca. 1870 on the site of a farmhouse that burned after the Civil War. The house in the above photo, taken in 2005, bears little resemblance to the original red brick house with the slate mansard roof built by George Walters.      (The Dabbiere Family)

Ashley and Alan Dabbiere enjoy history. They first looked at purchasing historic Hickory Hill in October of 2007. They fell in love with the property, as seen in the lower photograph taken during that visit, but they could not justify the enormous sales price of $25,000,000, considering the poor condition of the house and grounds.                    (Both: The Dabbiere Family)

Both of these photographs show the very large extension added to the south side of the house. A partial view of the newly created guest house can be seen to the right in the lower picture.

(Both: The Dabbiere Family)

An enormous three-year project to remodel Hickory Hill began in 2010. Both photos illustrate the removal of the south wing for the construction of a much larger addition.

(Both: The Dabbiere Family)

Ashley and Alan Dabbiere (left) are shown inspecting the renovations of the formal living room with some of the architects and builders. (The Dabbiere Family)

Shown above is the newly created brick paved vehicular circle driveway in front of the house. The large landscape urn in the center was moved from a location near the front of the house not too far from the flagpole. This is the same outdoor urn that Justice Jackson asked to be conveyed with the house when he purchased Hickory Hill in 1941.          (Carole Herrick)

The Dabbiere family is enjoying a moment at Hickory Hill after its completed renovation. From left to right: Alan, Calvin, Alston, Cameron, Constance and Ashley.

(The Dabbiere Family)

Both photos show the former barn for horses. Today the lower level is used for storage and the top section has been converted into office space for Alan.　　(Both: The Dabbiere Family)

These are two photos of the renovated Hickory Hill taken from the south entrance to the property off Chain Bridge Road. The driveway branches: the right side runs to the garages and the left side leads to the new circular driveway in front of the house.

(Both: The Dabbiere Family)

These two photos show Hickory Hill in 2016. Of interest is the renovated and significantly expanded extension to the south wing (right). The walkway leading to the front steps has been greatly reduced in length to make room for the newly designed paved brick circular driveway. The lawn urn has been moved so that it now stands prominently in the middle of the circle as seen in the above photo. (Both: Carole Herrick)

The newly created guest house is shown in the background to the right of the expanded south wing addition. (Carole Herrick)

Hickory Hill was built on top of a knoll facing Chain Bridge Road. This is a view of the house as seen from its south side. Note how the lawn slopes towards the driveway that leads to the garages.
(Carole Herrick)

# NOTES AND OPINIONS
## CHAPTER 1

Over the years there have been several descriptions of the road leading from the Chain Bridge to Fairfax City and beyond. Often it depended upon which direction, or where, one was traveling. During Langley's formative years, the road was known by some of the following names: the Falls Bridge Road, the road to the Little Falls, the road to Chain Bridge, the road to the Court House, the Langley-Fairfax Road, the road to Langley or the road to Lewinsville. By the early 1900s, it was often described as the Fairfax Highway or the Lewinsville-Langley Highway. This old highway is today's Chain Bridge Road. To simplify matters the Falls Bridge Road name is consistently used up to the Speer residency; from then on, the road is always called Chain Bridge Road.

## CHAPTER 4

On page 28 Major Woodward describes the Federal advance into Langley and mentions a rebel named Mr. Cook as fleeing the area when the soldiers arrived. The author is referring to Captain James Wallace Cooke, a native of North Carolina, who owned two separate parcels of land in the Langley area totaling 103 acres. Cooke served in the U.S. Navy, but in June of 1861 he resigned his U.S. Naval commission and joined the Confederate navy. He actually left Langley several months before General McCall's division arrived and never returned. His house was occupied by Federal troops, who vandalized it and destroyed his farm. His property was later turned into a contraband camp known as Camp Wadsworth.

## CHAPTER 5

There is no record concerning the departure of William "Billy" Means as Langley's postmaster in 1867. At that time he would have been 72 years of age. If Means had died, presumably he would have been buried beside his wife, Mary, in the Lewinsville Cemetery. But this is not the case: there is no William Means in the Lewinsville Cemetery. Did he remain in Langley, or did he move elsewhere? Means is not listed in the 1870 U.S. Federal Census, so he probably died before it was taken. Unfortunately, the whereabouts of Means after March 28, 1867 remains unknown.

How fortunate it is that an artist had the interest to do an oil painting of the original Hickory Hill as constructed by George Walters after the Civil War. The colorful painting clearly portrays the red-brick house and its mansard-style roof with the cupola on top. It is even more fortunate that Lillian Walters, a Walters by marriage, took the initiative in 1977 to send a photo of the painting to Ethel Kennedy. Later, the Dabbiere family produced a copy from the original painting, still in the Walters' family, for display in their historical room. The picture on page 52 is a black and white photograph taken of the Dabbiere's painting. Kennedy saved the letter. It is printed on the following page, giving an incorrect probable date of 1863 for the construction of the house:

"Dear Mrs. Kennedy:

I thought you might be interested in the enclosed picture which was taken from and original oil painting of Hickory Hill back, I believe, about 1863 or thereabout. My deceased husband Milton C. Walters was born at Hickory Hill in June of 1901 and his father Ulysses S. Walters was also born at Hickory Hill in August 1863. How old the plantation was at that time I do not know. My husband and his family moved from Hickory Hill around 1915 and the property was sold to a family by the name of Speer. The original oil painting was willed to my son Jack Walter about fifteen years ago and as you can imagine he is very proud of it and it occupies a prominent place in his living room of his Annandale, Va home.

You have made Hickory Hill such a beautiful show place and have given it quite a place of prominence. I took this picture several weeks ago for a member of the Speer family and it occurred to me at that time that you would be interested in it also. My best regards to you and your family.

Sincerely,
(Mrs.)Lillian L. Walters

May 28, 1977"

## CHAPTER 9

The *Washington Post* story beginning on page 79, describing extensive remodeling done to Hickory Hill, indicated that the one-room living room was divided into two separate rooms by the Jacksons. Based on other readings that were not primary sources, the author feels that this division is incorrect. It was the other way around: the Jacksons took two rooms and made them into one.

# SOURCES

## CHAPTER 1
### The Early Years and the Lee Family

1. Smith. *The General Historie.* Page 58.
2. Sweig, *Fairfax County, Virginia: A History.* Page 5.
3. *Ibid.*
4. *Ibid.* Page 7.
5. *Ibid.* Page 9.
6. *Ibid.*
7. Kilmer. *The Fairfax Family in Fairfax County.* Page 80.
8. Mitchell. *Beginning at a White Oak.* Page 202.
9. *Ibid.*
10. Hening. *Laws of Virginia.* Volume V. Page 143.
11. Harrison. Page 145.
12. Lee. *Lee Chronicle.* 71.
13. *Ibid.* Page 72.
14. *Ibid.*
15. Anderson. *Salona: Fairfax County Virginia.* Page 6.
16. Lee. *Ibid.* Page 88.
17. *Ibid.* Page 89.
18. *Ibid.* Page 50.
19. *Washington Federalist.* March 15, 1806.
20. Fairfax County Deed Book. J-2: page 84.
21. *Ibid.* J-2:18.
22. *Ibid.* J-2: 245.
23. *Ibid.* L-2:144
24. *Ibid.* L-2:149
25. *Ibid.* L-2:179.
26. *Ibid.* L-2:404.
27. *Alexandria Gazette.* November 15, 1811.
28. Fairfax County Deed Book. L-2: page 368.
29. *Ibid.* L-2: page 416.

## CHAPTER 2
### Maffitt and Salona

1. Anderson. Ibid. Page 10.
2. *Ibid.*
3. Brockett. Page 100.
4. *Alexandria Gazette.* May 7, 1803.
5. Fairfax County Will Book. J -1: page 241.
6. *Alexandria Gazette.* November 19, 1802.
7. Fairfax County Will Book. J–1: page 338.
8. Ibid.

9. *National Register of Historic Places Inventory Nomination.* Page 5.

10. Lee. *Ibid.* Page 290.

11. *Fairfax County Road Orders: 1749-1800.* Pages 103,118, 119,132.

12. Letters of Dolley Madison. Library of Congress.

13. Ibid.

14. Jones. *American State Papers.* Page 576 .

15. Jones. *Ibid.* Page 577.

16. Jennings. *A Colored Man's Reminiscences of James Madison.* Page 12.

17. *Washington Star.* 1905.

18. Jennings. *Ibid.* Page 13.

19. Booth. *Letter and Communication to Commodore Thomas Tingey from Mordecai Booth, His Clerk.* Page 19.

20. Jennings. *Ibid.* Page 13. Booth. *Ibid.* Page 20.

21. Booth. *Ibid.*

22. Booth. *Ibid.* Page 22.

23. Booth. *Ibid.*

24. Madison to Monroe. *The Writings of James Madison.* Page 298.

25. Monroe. *The Political Writings of James Monroe.* Page 465.

26. Smith. *Forty Years of Washington Society.* Page 98.

27. Sayrs. *Childhood in 1812 – A True Story.*

28. Smith. *Ibid.*

29. Love. *Lee Chronicle.* Page 292.

30. Fairfax County Will Book I: page 294.

31. Ibid. Page 302. Database of Washington D. C. Marriages to 1825.

32. Gambel. *Sully.* Page 59.

33. Fairfax County Deed Book V-2: page 85.

34. Maffitt tombstone. Lewinsville Cemetery, McLean, Virginia.

35. Fairfax County Deed Book Z-2: page 404.

36. Fairfax County Deed Book C-3: page 314.

37. *Ibid* E-3: page 399.

38. Fairfax County Will Book Q-1: page 271.

39. *Ibid.* Q-1: page 273.

40. *Ibid.* Q-1: page 331.

41. Anderson. *Ibid.* Page26.

42. Mackall, Sally Somerville. *Early Days of Washington.* Page 87.

43. Fairfax County Deed. Z-2: page 403.

44. *Ibid.*

45. *Ibid.* Page 406.

47. *Ibid.* C-3:314.

46. United States Federal Census 1840 and 1850.

47. Fairfax County Deed Book G-3: page 378.

48. *Ibid.* H-3: page 400.

49. *Ibid.* J-3: page 262.

50. *Ibid.* K-3: page 32.

51. *Ibid.* K-3: page 111.

# CHAPTER 3
## Langley's Early Years and the Walters Family

1. *National Register of Historic Places Registration Nomination Form.* Page 9
2. *Ibid.* Page 10.
3. *Ibid.* Page 9.
4. Fairfax County Deed Book E-3: page 234.
5. *Ibid.* G-3: page 381.
6. *National Register of Historic Places Registration Nomination Form.* Page 12.
7. Curran. *McLean Remembers.* Page 9.
8. Fairfax County Court Order Book 1842. Page 394.
9. *Code of Virginia, 1849.* "Taverns." Page 443.
10. Fairfax County Court Order Book 1842-1860.
11. United States Census 1830 and 1840.
12. Interview with Douglass Mackall, III. Southern Claim #20471 W. L. Ashton.
13. *Fairfax County Post offices 1750-1890.* Page 1.
14. Stuntz. *Historical Society of Fairfax County, Virginia.* Volume 14. Page 37.
15. United States Federal Census, 1900.
16. Fairfax County Deed Book L-2: page 389.
17. Helman. *Kenmore Vienna, Virginia: A History.*
18. Stuntz. *This Was Vienna, Virginia.* Page 90.
19. Helman. *Ibid.*
20. Fairfax County Deed Book H-3: page 121.
21. *Ibid.* Page 122.
22. Rosemary Goodman. Letter to Ethel Kennedy, December 6, 1963.
23. Fairfax County Deed Book D-3: page 170.
24. Fairfax County Deed Book W-2: page 15.
25. Fairfax County Deed Book L-4: page 310.
26. *Ibid.*
27. *National Register of Historic Places Nomination Form Langley Fork Historic District.*
28. Cook. *The History of Old Georgetown Pike.* Page 35. Curran. *McLean Remembers Again.* Page 37.
29. *Alexandria Gazette.* October 9, 1852.
30. *Baltimore Sun.* November 27, 1857.
31. *Alexandria Gazette.* August 21, 1848.
32. *Ibid.* September 16, 1848.
33. *Ibid.* August 17, 1852.
34. Fairfax County Deed Book S-3; page 61.
35. *Ibid.* U-3: page 19.
36. *Ibid.* B-4: page 104.
37. Fairfax County Land/Tax Books 1857: reel 433.
38. *Alexandria Gazette.* April 22, 1859.
39. United Stated Federal Census 1860.
40. Sprouse. Page 236.
41. *Ibid.* Page 237.

42. Stuntz. *Historical Society of Fairfax County, Virginia*. Volume 14. Page 39.

## CHAPTER 4
## Langley, The Walters Family and Civil War

1. Conley. Page 68.
2. *Ibid.*
3. Link. Page 3.
4. Woodward. Page 59.
5. *Ibid.* Page 44.
6. *Official Records*. Series I. Volume 5. Page 650.
7. Woodward. Page 45.
8. *New York Times*. October 11, 1861.
9. *Ibid.* October 10, 1861.
10. *Ibid.* October 30, 1861.
11. Johnson. *Brothers and Cousins: Confederate Soldiers and Sailors of Fairfax County, Virginia*. Page 111.
12. *Ibid.*
13. Evans, Thomas. "Quaker Sam' Means and the Loudoun Rangers." *Northern Virginia Heritage*. Volume VI. October 1984. Page 11.
14. Mackall Papers. "The Mackall Family and Their Connections." Virginia Room Fairfax County Public Library.
15. *Ibid.*
16. Mott Hooton Papers. Chester County Pennsylvania Historical Society.
17. *Official Records*. Series I. Volume V. Page 476.
18. *Ibid.* Page 489.
19. *Ibid.*
20. *Ibid.* Page 494.
21. Woodward. Page 57.
22. *Ibid.* Page 52.
23. *Ibid.* Page 62.
24. Letter Major Samuel K. Wilson. March 31, 1863. National Archives.
25. Captain Young to Colonel Henry. H. Wells. October 1, 1863. National Archives.
26. Papers Lorraine Holdsworth.

## CHAPTER 5
## Hickory Hill

1. Gott, Stuntz, and Triplett. *The Historical Society of Fairfax County Virginia*. Volume XIV. Page 33.
2. United States Federal Census. District of Columbia. 1870.
3. *Fairfax County Minute Book 1863-1867*. Page 93.
4. *Georgetown Pike: National Register of Historic Places Registration Form*. Page 14.
5. Sherman to Sherman. *Yearbook*. Volume 27. Page 101.
6. Fairfax County Court Order Book 1864. Page 69.
7. Goodman. *Ibid.*

8. *Ibid.*

9. Fairfax County Land Tax Records, 1864, 1868, and 1870.

10. Application of George F. M. Walters for Remittance of Taxes, Fairfax County, 1865.

11. Fairfax County Land Tax Records, 1864, 1868, and 1870.

12. "Surveys for Military Defenses of Northern Virginia and Vicinity of Washington:" August 1, 1862.

13. Library of Congress.

14. Fairfax County Deed Book H-4: page 266.

15. *Ibid.*

16. *Ibid.*

17. Fairfax County Deed Book R-4: page 33.

18. *Ibid.*

19. *Ibid.*

20. Fairfax County Deed Book B -5: page 277.

21. Goodman. *Ibid.*

22. *Alexandria Gazette.* June 21, 1870.

23. *Ibid.* April 11, 1871.

24. *Ibid.* September 10, 1872.

25. United States Southern Claims Commission Allowed Claims.

26. *Evening Star.* June 13, 1871.

27. National Archives. *Consolidated Index of Claims.* Page 244.

28. Stephenson. *The Cartography of Northern Virginia.* "Atlas of Fifteen Miles around Washington, 1879." Page 95.

29. *The Historical Society of Fairfax County: Yearbook.* Volume 5. Page 33.

30. *Ibid.* Page 32.

31. Mackall. *Fairfax County Stories 1607-2007.* Page 94.

32. *Ibid.* Page 98.

33. *Langley Fork Historic District.* 1980. Page 9.

34. *Historical Society of Fairfax County: Yearbook.* Volume 4. Page 2.

35. *Fairfax Herald.* March 8, 1889.

36. Fairfax County Deed Book L-5: page 359.

37. *Ibid.*

38. *Fairfax Herald.* May 24, 1889.

39. *Evening Star.* October 27, 1899.

40. *Ibid.* February 24, 1890.

41. Fairfax County Will Book J-5: page 198.

42. *Ibid.*

43. Fairfax County Deed Book W-4: page 131.

44. Fairfax County Will Book J-5: page 198.

45. *Fairfax Herald.* June 8, 1900.

46. Logical Book 147. Plat Book 5: Page 115.

47. Harwood. *Rails to the Blue Ridge.* Page 41.

48. *Ibid.* Page 35.

49. *Historical Society of Fairfax County, Virginia: Yearbook.* Volume 4. Page 13.

50. *Fairfax Herald.* December 15, 1905.

51. *Evening Star.* September 9, 1906.

52. Independent Mutual Fire Insurance Company. Fire Losses, 1906.
53. *Ibid.* Fire Losses, 1907.
54. *Fairfax Herald.* January 28, 1910.
55. *Evening Star.* May 16, 1907.
56. Fairfax County Deed Books C-7: page 679 and Q-7: page 637
57. Fairfax County Deed Book Z-7: page 507.
58. Stuntz. *This Was Virginia 1900-1927.* Page 9.
59. *Evening Star.* "With the Rambler." August 2, 1914.
60. *Ibid.*
61. Fairfax County Deed Book Z-7: page 507.
62. Fairfax County Deed Book M-8: page 579.

## CHAPTER 6
### The Speer Residency

1. Attachment. Circuit Court Papers. March Term, 1914. Walters vs. Walters.
2. Fairfax County Deed Book: Z-7: page 507
3. *Daughters of the Confederacy.* Salyer-Lee Chapter #1417. Virginia Division.
4. Circuit Court Papers Fairfax County, Virginia, May 3, 1922.
5. *Ibid.*
6. *Ibid.*
7. *Ibid.*
8. *Ibid.*
9. *Ibid.*
10. *Ibid.*
11. *Ibid.*
12. *Ibid.*
13. *Ibid.*
14. Fairfax County, Virginia, Will Book 10: page 209.
15. *The Washington Post.* January 14, 1923.
16. Fairfax County, Virginia, Will Book 10: page 209.
17. *Ibid.*
18. *Evening Star.* March 23, 1924.
19. Fairfax County Deed Book J-9: page 344.
20. *Ibid.* H-9: page 102.
21. *Washington Post.* March 22, 1925.
22. Grovermann to Kennedy. June 20, 1998.

## CHAPTER 7
### The Lyon/Fitch Years

1. Lee. "A History of Arlington County, Virginia." Page 35.
2. Rose. *Arlington County, Virginia: A History.* Page 156.
3. *Ibid.* Page 19.
4. *Ibid.* Page 12.
5. *Ibid.* Page 50.

6. Arlington County Deed Book 110: page 263.

7. Rose. *The Arlington Historical Magazine*. Volume 5. Page 51.

8. *Ibid*.

9. *New York Times*. October 19, 1911.

10. *Richmond Times Dispatch*. May 27, 1917.

11. Rose. *Ibid*. Page 55.

12. *Washington Post*. May 18, 2012.

13. *Ibid*.

14. Fairfax County Deed Book K-8: page 427.

15. *Ibid*. J-7: page 607.

16. *Ibid*. J-8: page 461.

17. *Ibid*. J-8: page 462.

18. *Ibid*. K-8: page 427.

19. *Old Dominion Citizens' Association: Neighborhood Conservation Plan*. Page 9.

20. Fairfax County Deed Book Z-8: page 445.

21. Rose. *Ibid*. Page 57.

22. *Herndon Observer*. February 11, 1926.

23. Templeman Collection. Arlington County Public Library Virginia Room.

24. *Fairfax Herald*. June 3, 1932.

25. Rose. *Ibid*. Page 52.

26. Fairfax County Deed Book J-9: page 344.

27. Fairfax County Deed Book S-9: page 181

28. Fairfax County Deed Book S-9: page 182.

29. *Ibid*. S-9: page 179.

30. *Fairfax Herald*. September 23, 1927.

31. Fairfax County Deed Book U-10: page 167.

32. *Fairfax Herald*. June 3, 1932.

33. *Ibid*. U-1:380

34. Bittinger. "Lyon Family Information."

35. *Washington Post*. September 7, 1936.

36. Fairfax County Historic Building Inventory. No. 38.

37. Fairfax County Deed Book B-12: page 208

38. *Ibid*. J-12: page 275

39. Curran. *McLean Remembers Again*. Page 28.

## CHAPTER 8
### The Rocca Residency

1 *Washington Post*. November 12, 1987.

2. *Ibid*. November 6, 1921.

3. *Ibid*.

4. *Evening Star*. June 1, 1924.

5. *Washington Post*. August 12, 1987.

6. *Evening Star*. April 21, 1930.

7. *Ibid*. January 28, 1934.

8. *Ibid*. March 18, 1934.

9. *Washington Post.* November 11, 1934.
10. *Ibid.* September 17, 1941.
11. *Ibid.* March 16, 1930.
12. Fairfax County Deed Book J-12: page 275.
13. Interview with Leo Rocca, Jr.
14. National Weather Service.
15. *Washington Post.* March 20, 1936.
16. *Ibid.* May 30, 1936.
17. *Ibid.* April 28, 1937.
18. *Ibid.* June 18, 1938.
19. Fairfax County Deed Book Z-14: page 508.
20. *Evening Star.* July 17, 1941.

## CHAPTER 9
## The Jackson Residency

1. *Washington Post.* January 7, 1940.
2. *Ibid.* June 3, 1941.
3. *Ibid.* June 13, 1941.
4. *Ibid.* June 15, 1941.
5. *Ibid.*
6. Papers of Leo Rocca, Jr.
7. *Washington Post.* July 8, 1941.
8. Barrett. "Buying Hickory Hill (1941)."
9. Yancey. *The Judge Advocate Journal.* Page 5.
10. Papers of Leo Rocca, Jr.
11. *Washington Post.* August 9, 1941.
12. Herrick. *100 Recollections of McLean & Great Falls, Virginia.* "Henry Smoot."
    Page 386.
13. *Washington Post.* June 23, 1943.
14. Herrick. *Ibid.* " Philip Graves." Page 150.
15. *Washington Post.* November 21, 1943.
16. Interview Tom Loftus III.
17. *Washington Post.* May 3, 1945.
18. *New York Times.* November 22, 1945.
19. *Washington Post.* March 19, 1946.
20. *New York Times.* October 2, 1946.
21. Interview Tom Loftus III.
22. *Washington Post.* September 29, 1952.
23. Herrick. *Ibid.* "David Shonerd." Page 379.
24. Herrick. *Ibid.* "Dariel Knauss Van Wagoner." Page 425.
25. *Washington Post.* October 13, 1954.
26. *Ibid.*
27. Fairfax County Will Book 50: page 244.
28. Fairfax County Deed Book 1368: page 398.

## CHAPTER 10
## The John and Jacqueline Kennedy Residency

1. Schlesinger. *A Thousand Days*. Page 86.
2. Curran. *McLean Remembers Again*. Page 35.
3. Fairfax County Deed Book 1542: page 385.
4. Ibid.
5. *Washington Post*. December 5, 1968.

## CHAPTER 11
## The Robert and Ethel Kennedy Residency

1. *Virginia Living*. October, 2005. *Times Community Newspapers*. March 2, 2005.
2. *Ibid.*
3. *Ibid.*
4. Kennedy. "A Mother with Moxie: A New Documentary Explores the Life of Ethel Kennedy by Her Filmmaker Daughter."
5. Schlesinger. *A Thousand Days: John F. Kennedy in the White House*. Page 695.
6. *Washington Post*. June 21, 1970.
7. " Hickory Hill," A film by George Plimpton and Robert Leacock, 1968.
8. *Washington Post*. May 22, 1978.
9. *Ibid.* May 22, 1967.
10. Greene, Roberta. "Oral History Interview with Art Buckwald."
11. *Look Magazine*. May 19, 1964
12. *Washington Post*. September 19, 1962.
13. *Ibid.* January 25, 1962.
14. *Ibid.*
15. *Ibid.* February 2, 1962.
16. *Time*. June 21, 2007
17. Herrick. *Ibid.* "Gary Heath." Page 196.
18. *Washington Post*. August 27, 1964.
19. Fairfax County Deed Book 2567: page 632.
20. *Washington Post*. September 4, 1964.
21. *Ibid.*
22. Neel, Sam. "A Brief History of the Ballantrae Ski Club 1964-1968." February 2000.
23. Fairfax County Circuit Court Papers: Case 14845.
24. *Ibid.*
26. State of West Virginia Certificate, Shenadoah Downs, Charles Town, August 1962.
27. *St. Petersburg Times*. December 31, 1966.
28. Fairfax County Circuit Court Papers: Case 14845.
29. *Washington Post*. March 17, 1968.
30. *New York Times*. March 13, 1968.
31. *Washington Post*. March 17, 1968.
32. Papers Lyndon B. Johnson Library. Television speech. October 31, 1968.
33. *Washington Post*. June 6, 1968.
34. *Ibid.*

35. *Ibid.*
36. *New York Times.* June 6, 1968.
37. *Ibid.* June 7, 1968.
38. *Ibid.* June 8, 1968.
39. *Ibid.* June 9, 1968.
40. *Ibid.*
41. *Ibid.*
42. *Washington Post.* August 14, 1973.
43. *Ibid.* April 26, 1984.
44. *Ibid.* December 31, 1997.
45. The Dabbiere Family.
46. Curran. *McLean Remembers Again.* Page 35.
47. The Dabbiere Family.
48. *Washington Life Magazine.* December, 2003.
49. Fairfax County Deed Book; page 1506.

## CHAPTER 12
### The Dabbiere Residency

1. Interview with Alan and Ashley Dabbiere.
2. Fairfax County Deed Book 10850: page 1438.
3. Interview with Alan and Ashley Dabbiere.
4. The *New York Times.* May 27, 2007.
5. Fairfax County Deed Book 20850: page 1506.
6. Fairfax County Deed Book 20944: page 1711.
7. Metropolitan Regional Information Systems, Inc. 2010.
8. Fairfax County Department of Planning and Zoning.
9. *Ibid.*
10. Interview with Alan and Ashley Dabbiere.
11. *Ibid.*

# BIBLIOGRAPHY

Barrett, John Q. "The Jackson List." http://thejacksonlist.com/.

Bittinger, Mary. "Lyon Family Information." Virginia Room. Fairfax County Public Library Archives.

Brockett, F. L. *The Lodge of Washington: A history of the Alexandria Washington Lodge No 22.* G. H. Ramey & Son: Alexandria, 1899.

Catlin, Martha. *A Historical Study of the McLean Community.* Manuscript Draft, 1988.

Clarke, Thurston. *The Last Campaign.* Henry Holt and Company: New York, 2008.

Conley, Brian. *Fractured Land: Fairfax County's Role in the Vote for Secession, May 23, 1861.* Fairfax County Public Library: Fairfax, 2001.

Curran, Louise C. and Curran, William. *McLean Remembers.* The Sound Publications: Vienna, Virginia, 1997.

Curran, Louise C. *McLean Remembers Again.* The Sound Publications: McLean, 1976.

Fairfax County Board of Supervisors. *Industrial and Historical Sketch of Fairfax County, Virginia.* 1907.

Fairfax County Board of Supervisors. *Langley Fork Historic District.* 1980.

Fairfax County 2007 Community Citizen Planning Committee. *Fairfax County Stories 1607-2007.* Fairfax County, 2007.

Gamble, Robert. *Sully.* Sully Foundation, Limited: Chantilly, Virginia, 1973.

Gott, Stuntz, and Triplett. *Historical Society of Fairfax County Virginia, Inc.* Volume XIV. Baptie Studios: Annandale, Virginia, 1976.

Greene, Roberta. "Oral History Interview with Art Buckwald." John Fitzgerald Kennedy Library, 1969.

Harrison, Fairfax. *Landmarks of Old Prince William,* Volumes I and II. Prince William County Historical Commission, 1987.

Harwood, Herbert, Jr. *Rails to the Blue Ridge.* Northern Virginia Regional Park Authority: Fairfax Station, Virginia, 2000.

Hellman, Susan. *Kenmore, Vienna, Virginia: A History.* Susan Holway Hellman, 2009.

Hening, William Waller. *Laws of Virginia.* University Press of Virginia: Charlottesville, 1969.

Herrick, Carole. *100 Recollections of McLean & Great Falls, Virginia.* Higher Education Publications: Reston, 2007.

Kennedy, John F. *Profiles in Courage.* Harper & Row: New York, 1964.

Kilmer, Kenton and Donald Sweig. *The Fairfax Family in Fairfax County.* Fairfax County of Comprehensive Planning: Fairfax, 1975.

Jennings, Paul. *A Colored Man's Reminiscences of James Madison.* George C. Beadle: Brooklyn, 1865. Special Collections, James Madison University Carrier Library.

Johnson, William Page, II. *Brothers and Cousins: Confederate soldiers and Sailors of Fairfax County, Virginia.* Iberian Publishing Company: Athens, Georgia.

Jolly, Bruce. *A Century of Progress.* Newsletter Press: Silver Spring, Maryland, 1990.

Lee, Cazenove Gardner, Jr. *Lee Chronicle.* Vantage Press: New York, 1957.

Link, Kenneth. *Northern Virginia Heritage "Courage and Betrayal: The Union Loyalists in Lewinsville."* George Mason University. February, 1986.

Mackall, Sally Somerville. *Early Days of Washington.* G. E. Bishop Printing Company: Sterling, Illinois, 1899.

Mills, Gary B. *Southern Loyalists in the Civil War: The Southern Claims Commission.* Genealogical Publishing Company: Baltimore, 1994.

Mitchell, Beth. *Beginning at a White Oak: Patents and Northern Neck Grants of Fairfax County, Virginia.* McGregor and Werner, 1977.

Netherton, Nan and Ross. *Arlington County in Virginia: A Pictorial History.* The Donning Company: Norfolk, VA, 1987.

Netherton, Sweig, Artemel, Hickin and Reed. *Fairfax County, Virginia: A History.* Fairfax County Board of Supervisors: Fairfax, Virginia, 1978.

Plimpton, George and Leacock, Robert. "Hickory Hill." Pennebaker Hegedus Films, 1968.

Rose, Ruth. "Role of Frank Lyon and His Associates in the Early Development of Arlington County." *The Arlington Historical Magazine.* Volume V. Arlington Historical Society: Arlington, 1976.

Schlesinger, Arthur, Jr. *A Thousand Days: John F. Kennedy in the White House.* Houghton Mifflin Company: Boston, 1965.

Smith, Gene A., *Thomas ap Catesby Jones.* Naval Institute Press: Annapolis.

Smith, John Captain. *The General Historie of Virginia, New England and the Summer Ifles, 1624.* The Anglia Company, Historical Reproductions: Hinesville, Georgia.

Stephenson, Richard, *The Cartography of Northern Virginia: Facsiimile Reproductions of Maps Dating From 1608 to 1915.* History and Archaeology Section Office of Comprehensive Planning, Fairfax, Virginia, 1983.

Stuntz, Mayo. "Development of Postal Service in Fairfax County, Virginia, 1750–1890." *Historical Society of Fairfax County, Virginia, Inc.* Volume 14. Baptie Studios: Annandale, 22003.

Stuntz, Connie Pendleton and Stuntz, Mayo Sturdevant. *This Was Virginia 1900 – 1927: As Shown by the Glass Negatives of J. Harry Shannon, The Rambler.* Hallmark Publishing Company: Gloucester Point, Virginia, 1998.

Stuntz, Mayo and Robert Lisbeth. *Fairfax County Post Offices 1750-1890.* Springfield Stamp Club: Springfield, VA, 1985.

Templeman, Eleanor Lee. *Arlington Heritage: Vignettes of a Virginia County.* Avenel Books: New York, 1959.

Townsend, George. *Campaign of a Non-Combatant.*

Woodward, Evan Morrison. *History of the Third Pennsylvania Reserve.* MacCrellish and Quigley: Trenton, 1883.

Yancey, Clarence Major (editor). *The Judge Advocate Journal.* Volume II. Judge Advocates Association: Washington D. C., 1945.

## COLLECTIONS

Henry C. Mackall Papers. The Virginia Room. Fairfax County Regional Public Library.
John Fitzgerald Kennedy Library
Mott Hooton Papers. Chester County Pennsylvania Historical Society.
Library of Congress
Lorraine Holdsworth Collection.
National Archives
Robert H. Jackson Center
Virginia Room, Arlington County Public Library
Virginia Room, Fairfax City Public Library

# NEWSPAPERS

*Alexandria Gazette*
*Baltimore Sun*
*Evening Star*
*Frank Leslie's Illustrated Newspaper*
*Fairfax Herald*
*Herndon Observer*
*McLean Providence Journal*

*National Intelligencer*
*New York Times*
*Northern Virginia Sun*
*Richmond Times Dispatch*
*The Sun Gazette*
*The Washington Post and Times Herald*
*Washington Federalist*

# MAGAZINES

*House & Garden*
*Harper's Weekly*

*Look*
*Washington Life Magazine*

# INDEX

Hutson, Samuel, 44,51
Hutson, Sarah Walters, 39,44,47,51
Hyannis Port, 96
Immaculate Heart Mission Fathers, 71
Independent Mutual Fire Insurance Company, 46
Ingleside, 44
"Inquiring Camera Girl," 91
Insull, Samuel, 77
International Brotherhood of Teamsters, 97
International Military Tribunal, 81, 86,90
Interstate 495, 10
Interstate Commerce Commission, 61
Iroquois, 1
Ivy Hill, 22
Izvestia, 112
Jackson, Irene, 73,77,78,79,80,83, 86,89,83,86,89,91,92
Jackson, Robert C., 15
Jackson, Robert H. Justice, 57,75, 77,78,79,80,81,82,83,84,85,86, 87,88,90,126
Jackson, William, 77,83
James River, 1
Jamestown High School, 77
Jamestown, New York, 77,83
Jamestown, Virginia, 1
James W. Walters, and complaints Vs. Katherine H. Walters, and Complaints, 47
Japan, 80
Jenkins, Henry, 29
Jennings, Edmund, 2
Jewish people, 82
John Milner Architects, 118
Johnson, Albert S. General, 30,34
Johnson, Joseph General, 31
Johnson, Lyndon, 100,101,113
Johnson property, 44
John Storm Farm, 44
Jones, Dr., 45
Jones family, 18,29
Jones, Mark, 29
Jones, Mary Walker Carter, 15,19
Jones, Patterson, 29
Jones, Thomas ap Catesby, 15,19,29
Judicial Procedures Reform Bill of 1937, 84
Kaderly, W.F., 45
Kane, Thomas Colonel, 31
Keating, Kenneth, 99,100
Keeley Cure, 54,60
Kenilworth Farm, 65,66
Kennedy, Christopher, 102
Kennedy, David, 102,107
Kennedy, Douglas, 102
Kennedy, Edward (Ted), 100,102, 114

Kennedy, Ethel Skakel, 39,41,56, 57,91,95,96,98,99,100,101,102, 103,106,107,108,109,115,116
Kennedy, Jacqueline Bouvier, 83,91
Kennedy, John Fitzgerald, 83,91,92, 97,98,99,101,106,108,111
Kennedy, John, Jr., 102
Kennedy, Joseph, 91,99,106
Kennedy, Joseph 2nd, 102,107,110
Kennedy, Kerry, 102,109
Kennedy, Mary Richardson, 103
Kennedy, Michael, 102
Kennedy, Robert (Bobby), 91,95,96, 97,98,99,100,101,102,103,106, 107,108,110,111,113,114,115, 117
Kennedy, Robert, Jr., 95,96,102, 103,107,110
Kennedy, Rose, 91,99
Khruschev, Nikita, 98,112
King, Martin Luther, Jr., 113
Kirby, Ward, 64
Kirkwood, 38
Krupt, Gustav, 83
La Guardia Airport, 102
Langdon, Mrs., 24
Langley, 2,8,14,19,21,22,24,25,26, 27,28,29,30,32,33,34,35,39,40, 43,44,45,46,47,55,64,76,77,78, 79,80,91,92,95,117,118
Langley Division Sons of Temperance, 24
Langley-Fairfax Road, 76
Langley Farm, 3,4,5,6,8,9
Langley Flats, 43,44
Langley Fork, 21,25,27,35,36,42, 49,50
Langley Fork National Register Historic District, 118
Langley Land Company, 38
Langley Lane, 83
Langley Methodist Church, 43
Langley Ordinary, 25,28,29,30,32, 35,36,39,41,43,44,45,47,52,92
Langley Post Office, 22,24,26,39,45
Langley School, 83
Langley Tavern, 22,23,24,25,23,36, 39,41,48
Langley Toll House, 21,36,43
Langley tract, 5
Leake, William Chaplain, 32
Lebowitz, Mortimer, 92
Lee, Alice, 2
Lee, Arthur, 2
Lee, Chapman, 16
Lee, Charles, 9
Lee, Elizabeth Collins, 4,5,6,9,10,21
Lee, Elizabeth Steptoe, 2
Lee, Flora, 2,12
Lee, Francis Lightfoot, 2
Lee, Francis Lightfoot, II, 4
Lee, Hannah, 2,11

Lee, Hannah Harrison Ludwell, 2
Lee, Henry, 8
Lee, Henry "Light Horse Harry," 2, 3,4,8,9,10
Lee, Henry IV "Black Horse," 2,3,8
Lee, Laura, 16
Lee, Lucy Grymes, 2,3
Lee, Ludwell, 2,3
Lee, Matilda Ludwell, 2,3,8
Lee, Philip, 2
Lee, Philip Ludwell, 2,3,8,12
Lee, Richard Bland, 3,4,5,6,9,10,21
Lee, Richard Henry, 2,4,11,14
Lee, Robert E. General, 8,33
Lee, Theodorick, 5,10
Lee, Thomas, 2,8,11,12
Lee, Thomas Ludwell, 2
Lee, William, 2
Leesburg, 5
Leeton, 11,12,14
Legion of Merit Award, 72
Leo Rocca, Inc., 74
Lewinsville, 28,29,32,44,45
Lewinsville Cemetery, 18,19,34,44, 45,46
Lewinsville-Falls Church Road, 66
Lewinsville, P.O., 45
Lewinsville Precinct, 27,30,39
Lewinsville Presbyterian Church, 18,19,44
Lewinsville Road, 50
Ley, Robert, 83
Lincoln, Abraham President, 27
Lincoln dealership, 78
Lincolnville, 44
Little Falls, 1,2,3,5,8,24,26,75
Little Falls Road, 4
Loftus, Thomas, Jr., 80,83
Loftus, Thomas III, 83
Loftus, William, 83
London, 81
London Charter, 81
Long Bridge, 61
Los Angeles, 101,102
Loudoun County, 21,22,25,31,56
Loudoun Rangers, 30
Love, Matilda Lee, 12,13,14
Love, Richard, 12,13
Loving, Sallie, 48,52
Lydecker's Precinct, 27,42
Lyon & Fitch, 62,63,64,65,66
Lyon, Frank, 56,57,59,61,62,63,64, 65,66,67,68,69,71,72,74,79
Lyon, Georgia (Georgie) Wright, 61,63,66,69,72,74,79
Lyonhurst, 63,64,71,72
Lyonhurst Avenue, 63
Lyon, John Lieutenant, 63,64,70
Lyon Park, 62,63,69
Lyon Properties, Inc., 62
Lyon's Addition to Clarendon, 62
Lyon Village, 57,64,69